4 Nc3 Gambit In The Queen's Gambit Accepted And Slav

A Repertoire For White

John L. Watson

1986

Coraopolis, Pennsylvania

Chess Enterprises, Inc.

ISBN 0-931462-53-3

Editor: B. G. Dudley

Diagrams and Proof Reading: Thomas Magar

Cover Design: E. F. Witalis, Jr.
              Witalis-Burke Associates
              Pittsburgh, Pennsylvania

Othe Chess Enterprises Books by John L. Watson:

    6...Nc6 in the Sämisch Variation, King's Indian Defense

    Taimanov & Knight's Tour Benoni

    Chessman Comics 2, Treachery in Transylvania

Introduction

Theoretical chess boks tend to grow as much after they're finished as before. In the case of the book before you, a rash of new material came in just as I'd finished a first draft. This is particularly interesting because 4 Nc3 versus the Queen's Gambit Accepted has not really been in vogue since the early 60's. Why now, then? Quite simply, White's frustration with the main lines of the Q.G.A. (both Classical and Modern) have led to a reevaluation of his alternatives. In this context, 3 e4 and 3 e3 have been played extensively, but it's becoming clear that neither move produces very interesting chess versus a well-prepared defender.

That's where 3 Nf3 and 4 Nc3 comes in. At the worst, this sequence guarantees a complicated middlegame with attacking chances. At best, he gets a devastating initiative. In this book, I have tried to give White a complete Q.G.A. repertoire, beginning with an analysis of Black's important third- and fourth-move alternatives and highlighted by a discussion of the complex gambit resulting from 3 Nf3 Nf6 4 Nc3 a6 5 e4 b5 6 e5, etc.. The last three chapters deal with the *related* gambit in the Slav Defense, 4...c6 5 e4 b5 6 e5, etc.. This is not as well-established as the line with 4...a6, but has also had good success.

There will inevitably be a number of controversial assessments in a book such as this, due to the many unclear (and even bizarre) positions. Often I have been content to set forth a sequence of exemplary moves, since exhaustive analysis was simply out of the question. Unfortunately, not much help will be found from the few writers who have dealt with this material elsewhere. What *has* been written tends to repeat references to well-known, useless games, while ignoring the obviously critical continuations. Here I should mention the exception, Cafferty and Hooper's book (see the bibliography), which does an excellent job of digging up ancient references to the irregular lines. Overall, however, I have seldom seen a variation with such enormous gaps between what grandmasters know and what the average player has available to set up a repertoire. This necessitates a certain amount of added material in a work I had hoped to limit. As a consequence, in fact, I had considered brushing aside the whole question of 4...c6 with a facile "This transposes to the Slav Defense." But the exciting lines with 5 e4 have received almost no attention, despite Kasparov's advocacy, and the reader will be well-rewarded by a look at its amazing ramifications.

This is my sixth project with Chess Enterprises, and I want to express my thanks to Bob Dudley. He puts more effort into producing his books than many authors do into writing theirs.

John Watson
Fairfax, California 1985

Bibliography

These few books and magazine comprised the bulk of my research, although of course many publications provided individual games and notes. The relevant material from sources such as Pachman, Euwe, and Taimanov has been passed on and incorporated in *ECO* and Cafferty and Hooper's book.

Chess Informant 1 - 39

A Complete Defence to 1 d4 (Pergamon 1981) Cafferty, Bernard & Hooper, David

Encyclopedia of Chess Openings D (Chess Informant 1976); ECO in the Text

Modern Grandmaster Chess (Chicago Chess Books 1974) Karklins, Andrew

Players Chess News

Tournament Chess

Symbols

†	Check
△	With the idea of
±	Some advantage to White, sometimes convertible to a win
±	Clear advantage to White, usually convertible to a win
±/±	An assessment between the above two symbols
±±	A clearly won position
=	The position is balanced or equal
∞	The position is complicated and unclear
!	Strong move
!!	Excellent move
!?	Interesting move
?!	Not the best move, although with some value (e.g. trickiness)
?	West move
??	Blunder
(!)	Probably a good move (e.g. could use more tests)
(?)	Probably a bad move (e.g. could use more tests)
½ - ½	Draw agreed
1 - 0	Black resigns
0 - 1	White resigns
(1 - 0,75	White went on to win in 75 moves
Ch	Championship
IZ	Interzonal
corres	Correspondence game

Contents

I	Black avoids 3...Nf6	6
II	3 Nf3 Nf6 4 Nc3: Odd Fourth Moves	15
III	4...a6: Introduction, 7...Bb7, and 7...Nb4	26
IV	4...a6 Gambit with 7...c6	32
V	4...a6 Gambit with 7...Nxc3	38
VI	4...c6: Introduction and 7...Bf5	49
VII	7...e6 Gambit with 11...Qd7	52
VIII	7...e6 Gambit with 11...g6	56
	Index of Variations	62

I Black Avoids 3...Nf6

Diagram 1

After 3 Nf3

The subject of this book is the Queen's Gambit Accepted, and in particular the variation **1 d4 d5 2 c4 dxc4 3 Nf3** (see the diagram) **3...Nf6 4 Nc3**. While 3...Nf6 is easily the most frequent choice in this line, Black does have a number of logical third-move options. Traditionally, with the exception of 3...a6, these moves have been considered inferior or at least unimportant, yet the written theory deals spottily and, I think, inadequately with them. We find the familiar problem that one well-known game is supposed to serve as a model, and yet the game bears little relation to correct play. In spite of this situation, the scanty use of anything but 3...Nf6 by leading GMs tends to indicate that they indeed find the alternatives wanting.

We examine: A **3...Bg4**; B **3...c5**; C **3...b5**; D **3...a6**. Others:

(a) **3...Nd7 4 e4 Nb6** (4...Nf6 5 Nc3 transposes to 4...Nd7 of Chapter II) **5 Ne5** (5 a4 a5 might also transpose to that line) **5...Nf6 6 Nc3 e6 7 Nxc4** with a nice advantage (Cafferty and Hooper);

(b) **3...c6 4 e4!? Nf6 5 Nc3 b5 6 e5** is the gambit analysed in Chapter VI - VIII. A better solution is **4 e3!**, when White will recapture the c4 pawn without the usual loss of tempo (i.e. Bd3/xc4): **4...Bg4** (4...b5 5 a4 -- see 3...b5 below) **5 Bxc4 e6 6 Nc3 Nd7** (6...Nf6 7 h3 Bh5 8 g4! Bg6 9 Ne5 Nbd7 10 Nxg6 hxg6 11 Bd2. White is a "half" tempo up on the normal 4 e3 Bg4 Q.G Q.G.A., due to Black's passive ...c6. Kan-Goldberg, USSR Ch 1952 continued 11...Be7 12 Qf3 a6 13 Bb3 Nb6 14 0-0-0 ±) **7 h3 Bh5 8 0-0 Ngf6 9 e4 Be7 10 Bg5 h6** (10...0-0 11 e5 Nd5 12 Bxe7 Qxe7 13 Ne4 ± ECO) **11 Be3 0-0 12 e5!?** (or more simply, 12 Be2 ± ECO) **12...Nd5 13 Nxd5 cxd5 14 Bd3** ± Antunac - Kovacevic, Yugoslavia 1975.

(c) **3...e6 4 e4 c5** (4...Nf6 5 Nc3 Bb4 6 Bg5 is the Vienna Defense to the Queen's Gambit, considered in some detail in Chapter II, B. Otherwise, 5 e5 Nd5 6 Bxc4 Bb4+ 7 Nbd2 is assessed as better for White by Cafferty and Hooper. This is almost always true in such positions with the Black queen's bishop still on c8) **5 Bxc4 cxd4 6 Nxd4 Nf6** (6...a6 7 Be3!) **7 Nc3**. This position favors White, and is found in Chapter II, C, note to 5 d5.

A

	3	Bg4
	4 Ne5	Bh5
	5 Nc3	

5 g4!? f6! is unclear.

Diagram 2

After 5 Nc3

5 ..... Nd7

(a) 5...f6!? is the most interesting try for activity; Tartakower gives 6 Nxc4 e6 (6...e5 7 dxe5 Qxd1+ 8 Nxd1 Nc6 9 exf6 Nxf6 "with some compensation" -- Minev; but I don't think so. Also 7 d5 is good) 7 Qb3 Nc6 (7...b6!?) 8 Qxb7 Nb4. Now Cafferty suggests that White is winning after 9 Qe4! Bg6 10 Qxe6+ and 11 Ne3. However, 9...Kf7! △...Bg6 is not so clear, e.g. 10 Ne3 Bg6 11 Qf3 Nge7 12 a3 Nbc6 13 d5 exd5 14 Ncxd5 Nxd5! etc.. They also give 8...Nxd4 "with reasonable play."

The real problem with all this is that White doesn't have to rush so when Black has central weaknesses. Hence 7 f3! Nc6 8 e3 (±) and Black has no plan, whereas White can build up by Be2, 0-0 and eventually e4.

(b) 5...e6? 6 g4 Bg6 7 h4 (±) 7...f6 8 Qa4+ c6 9 Nxg6 hxg6 10 Qxc4 Kf7 11 e4 Nd7 12 Be3 ± Alekhine - Grunfeld, Semmering 1926. Sometimes the only game quoted.

6 Qa4

White's central superiority also guarantees him a healthy edge after 6 Nxc4: 6...Ngf6 (6...c6 7 f3 △e4 is logical, but also 7 g3!? e6 8 Bg2 Ngf6 9 0-0 Be7 10 a4 gave White control of the game in Rubinstein - von Holzhausen, Hannover 1926) 7 Qb3 Nb6 8 e4! Qxd4 9 Be3 Qd7? (but 9...Qd8 10 f3 e6 11 Nb5 Nxc4 12 Qxc4 ± -- Bogoljubov; an odd place to stop, but 12...c6 13 Rd1 Qa5† 14 Bd2! Qxb5 15 Qxb5 cxb5 16 Bxb5† Nd7 17 Ba5! confirms the assessment) 10 Bxb6 axb6 11 Nxb6! ±± Bogoljubov - Grekov, Kiev 1914.

6 ..... c6

7 Qxc4

Alekhine gives 7 Nxd7 Qxd7 8 Qxc4 △e4 and Be3, also not bad.

7 ..... Nxe5

7...Nb6 8 Qd3 f6 9 Nc4 Nxc4 10 Qxc4 Bf7 11 Qa4 e5 12 dxe5 fxe5 or 12...Bc5 (Minev); but 12 dxe5 fxe5 13 g3 Nf6 14 Bh3 Bc5 15 0-0 favors White, as does 12...Bc5 13 g3 or even 13 e3.

8 dxe5 e6

9 g4!

Securing a huge spatial advantage. Taimanov now gives 9...Bg6 10 Bg2 Qc7 11 f4 "±". Cafferty and Hooper disagree, calling Black's position "cramped but defensible". I have to agree with Taimanov, in view of the threat 12 e4 and 13 f5, among other things. Black could try 11...h5 (11...Qb6

12 e4!), but 12 gxh5 Rxh5 13 Be3! cuts off his development, and here 12...
Qb6 13 Be3(!) Qxe3 14 Bxc6† also seems to work.

B

3	c5
4 d5!	

The other line is 4 e4!? cxd4 (4...e6 5 Nc3 cxd4 6 Qxd4 Bd7?! 7 Ne5!
Nf6 8 Nxc4 ±/± Miles - Korchnoi, Tilburg 1985) 5 Qxd4 (5 Bxc4!? Nc6 6
0-0 intends 6...e5 7 Ng5 Nh6 8 f4 with attack, but here 6...e6! must be met:
7 e5!?) 5...Qxd4 6 Nxd4 Bd7! (compare the similar endings with ...Nf6 in;
here Black need not worry about e5. 6...a6 7 Bxc4 e6 8 Be3 ±) 7 Bxc4
Nc6 8 Nxc6 (8 Be3 Nf6) 8...Bxc6 9 Nc3 e6 10 Nb5 Bb4† = Spassov - Osnos,
Plovdiv 1982. The text is more thematic.

4	e6

4...Nf6 5 Nc3 e6 6 e4! is 3...Nf6 4 Nc3 c5 5 d5 etc. of Chapter II, C.

5 Nc3	exd5

The only alternative (besides 5...Nf6 again) would be 5...a6!?, but 6 a4 Nf6
7 e4 exd5 8 e5 just works out better for White than in the corresponding
lines of Chapter 11, C, as does 6...exd5 7 Qxd5, for which compare what follows:

6 Qxd5	

6 Nxd5 (Cafferty and Hooper), but 6...Be6! △ 7 e4 Bxd5!.

6	Qxd5
7 Nxd5	Bd6

7...Kd8 8 e4!.

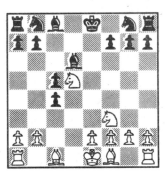

Diagram 3

After 7...Bd6

8 Nd2!?

A good alternative is 8 e4 Nc6 9 Bxc4 Nge7 10 0-0 "±" (ECO and C & H).
Here 9...Bg4 10 0-0 Bxf3 11 gxf3 also looks better for White.

8	Ne7
9 Nxc4	Nxd5
10 Nxd6†	Ke7
11 Nxc8†	Rxc8

White has achieved a riskless two-bishop-versus-two-knight ending. He has
two promising ways to proceed:

(a) 12 Bg5† f6 13 0-0-0 Rd8 (13...Nb4 14 Bf4 Nxa2† 15 Kb1 Nb4 16 e4
with a fine attack: ±/±) 14 e4!? fxg5 15 exd5 Rd6 16 Bc4!? (16 h4! ± looks

better) 16...Nd7 17 Rhe1† Kf6 18 b3 Ne5 19 Re4 Rad8 20 Rf1 Nxc4 21 bxc4 Gaprindashvili - Levitina, Candidates 1983 and now instead of 21...Ra6 22 Kb2 Rdd6 23 f4!, 21...b5! should certainly have been tried, when White presumably tries for an outside passed pawn with 22 cxb5, but this is not clear.

(b) 12 g3 Nc6 13 Bg2 Rd8 14 Bg5† f6 15 Bd2 Rd6 16 0-0 Rad8 17 Rac1 b6 18 Rfe1 (18 a3(!)) 18...Kf7 19 Bf1?! (19 a3!) 19...Nde7! 20 Bf4 Ne5 21 a3 a5 22 b4 cxb4 23 axb4 axb4 24 Bxe5 fxe5 25 Rb1 Nd5 26 e4 Nf6 27 Rxb4 Rd1 ½ - ½ Bellon - Seirawan, Zurich 1984.

In both of these endings, White had a small but definite advantage.

C

3 .....   b5

Diagram 4   After 3...b5

Readers who grew up with the many beginner's books which showed why 3...b5 was a grave error may be surprised to find that those books' analysis was quite wrong. Modern texts also dismiss it offhand, but in fact 3...b5 is playable. White must respond very accurately to maintain an edge.

                    4 a4

Or 4 e3 c6 5 a4, which transposes. Black also has the somewhat dubious 4 e3 Bd7?! 5 a4 c6 6 Ne5! △ 7 axb5 and 8 Qf3. Finally 4 e3 Nf6 5 a4 c6 6 axb5 cxb5 7 b3 e6 (7...Be6 8 bxc4 bxc4 9 Nc6 ±) transposes to the text.

                    4 .....   c6
                    5 e3

5 axb5 axb5 7 b3 e5! (Cafferty and Hooper), intending 7 Nxe5 Bb4†.

                    5 .....   e6

Others:

(a) 5...a6?! 6 b3! cxb3 7 axb5 cxb5 8 Bxb5† Bd7 9 Bxd7† Nxd7 10 Qxb3 (at least ±, due to the weak a-pawn) is old Philidor analysis, given by many theory books as the only 3...b5 line;

(b) 5...Qb6!? is much more interesting. It was worked out by Haberditz many years ago, an analysis rediscovered by Cafferty and Hooper: 6 axb5 cxb5 7 b3! (and not ECO's 7 Ne5 due to 7...e6! 8 Nxf7? -- but 8 Qf3 Qb7 -- 8...Kxf7 9 Qf3† Nf6 10 Qxa8 Bb4† 11 Bd2 Bxd2† 12 Nxd2 Nc6 etc.) 7...cxb3 8 Qxb3 b4 (? 8...e6 ±) 9 Qd5! Bb7 10 Bb5† Bc6 (10...Nc6 11 Ne5) 11 Ne5! e6 12 Qf3! Nf6 13 Ba4!! and suddenly Black can no longer hold his material!

6 axb5

6 b3?! a5! 7 bxc4 b4 is worse for White than what follows.

6 .....   cxb5
7 b3

Diagram 5   After 7 b3

7 .....   a5!

Very interesting too is 7...Bb4† 8 Bd2 Bxd2†. Now Cafferty and Hooper give "9 Nfxd2! (9 Nbxd2 c3)". But in fact, 9 Nfxd2(?) a5! 10 bxc4 b4 does not compare well with the text at all, Black having gotten rid of his bad bishop and forced the White pieces back. Instead, 9 Nbxd2! should be played, with 9...c3 10 Bxb5† Bd7 11 Bxd7† and 12 Ne4 ±, since the c-pawn cannot be held for long (Zabelle and Watson).

The text, 7...a5!, is better: 8 bxc4 b4 9 Ne5 Nf6 (9...Nbd7 10 Qa4!) 10 Bd3 Be7!? (10...Bd6! looks better, to break up the center) 11 0-0 0-0 12 Nd2 Bb7!? 13 f4 (±) 13...Nbd7 14 Qc2 and White was able to mount an effective attack on the a-pawn by c5, N2c4, and doubling on the a-file, Hybl - Ericson, 5th World Correspondence Ch 1965-68.

In general, this variation seems to favor White, but not so clearly as had been supposed.

D

3 .....   a6
4 e4!?

Diagram 6   After 4 e4

An attack first worked out by Borisenko. I recommend it as open-ended and exciting, although it should be admitted that this line has no clear theoretical status as yet. For those who want a safer alternative, 4 e3 with a main line "Modern" Q.G.A. after 4...Bg4 5 Bxc4 e6 6 0-0 (6 Qb3 Bxf3 7 gxf3 b5 is roughly equal), or with e.g. 4...e6 5 Bxc4 Nf6 and ...c5 (transposing to a Classical Q.G.A.), may be recommended. The point of playing 4 e4 is to avoid those line (whose theoretical status is rather good at the moment -- especially the Classical), and to substitute a vigorous attack for the relatively dry play which usually results from 4 e3. On the negative side, White must play some lines a pawn down, but that is a situation he may learn to feel comfortable with should he adopt 3 Nf3 Nf6 4 Nc3.

| 4 ..... | b5 |

Others from the diagram are less challenging, although insufficiently analyzed:

(a) 4...Bg4 5 Bxc4 e6 6 0-0 Nd7 (or 6...Nf6 7 Nc3 Be7 8 Qe2 0-0 9 Rd1 b5 10 Bb3 (±) 10...b4?! 11 Na4 ± Balanel - Lundin, Prague 1954; here 8... Bxf3 9 Qxf3 Qxd4? 10 e5! is practically winning for White) 7 Nc3 c4 8 d5! e5 9 a4 Bd6 10 Be2 (△Nd2-c4 ECO) 10...Bxf3 11 Bxf3 Ne7 12 Nb1 (! or, of course, 12 g3 ±) 12...0-0 13 Na3 Nc8 14 Bd2 Be7 15 a5 Nd6 16 b4 ± (at least) Borisenko - Flohr, USSR Ch 1950. Black never really had anything to compensate for White's space and two bishops.

(b) 4...Nf6 5 e5!? (5 Nc3 b5 6 e5 etc. is our main-line 4 Nc3 gambit of Chapters 3-5) 5...Nd5 6 Bxc4 b5! (Cafferty and Hooper suggest this to replace 6...e6 7 Nc3 Nxc3 8 bxc3 c5 9 0-0 Nc6 10 Qe2! Be7 11 Rd1 Qc7 12 Bg5 ± of Geller - Nilsson, Stockholm 1954. 6...Bf5 or 6...Bg4 fail to 7 Qb3!, and 6...Be6 7 Nbd2 is useless) 7 Bxd5 Qxd5

Diagram 7   After 7...Qxd5

Now C & H give 8 Nc3 Qc4 "with some hopes of play on the White squares". In fact, this looks quite reasonable for the second player. On the other hand, White could try 8 0-0(!), e.g. 8...Bg4 9 Nc3 Bxf3? 10 Nxd5 ±, or here 9...Qb7 10 d5 e6 11 h3! Bxf3 12 Qxf3 b4 13 Ne4 exd5 (13...Qxd5 14 Rd1 Qc6 15 Bg5 etc.) 14 Ng5 c6 15 e6 fxe6 16 Nxe6 etc.. Otherwise, 8 0-0 Bb7 9 Nc3 Qc4 10 Be3 △ Rc1 and 8...b4 9 a3 (9 h3!?) 9...Bg4 10 axb4 Bxf3 11 gxf3 Nc6 12 Qa4 are certainly better for White.

(c) 4...c5 5 Bxc4 (On 5 d5, 5...Nf6 is possible, and 5...b5(!) 6 a4 Bb7 [6... Nf6!? 7 axb5 Nxe4 8 Bxc4 Nd6 9 Nbd2 unclear] 7 b3!? Nf6 looks fine for Black) 5...cxd4 (5...e6!?; then 6 a4 seems best) 6 Nxd4 (or 6 Qxd4 ±, e.g. 6... Qxd4 7 Nxd4 e6 8 Be3 Nf6 9 f3 b6 10 Nd2 Bb7 11 Kf2 ± Taimanov - Nei, USSR 1964) 6...e5?! (but 6...e6 7 Nc3 or 7 0-0 is the kind of ± we've seen elsewhere -- development and space) 7 Qa4†! Qd7 (7...Bd7 8 Qb3 Qe7 9 0-0!

Nc6 [9...exd4 10 Qxb7 Bc6 11 Qc8† Qd8 12 Bxf7†] 10 Qxb7 Rb8 11 Nxc6 etc.; 7...Nd7 8 Nf5, e.g. 8...g6 9 Bxf7†! Kxf7 10 Qb3† Kf6 11 h4! ECO) 8 Bb5 axb5 9 Qxa8 Qxd4 10 Qxb8 Bb4† 11 Nc3! Qxe4† (11...Bxc3† 12 bxc3 Qxc3† 13 Bd2! Qxa1† 14 Ke2 Qd4 15 Qxc8† ±) 12 Be3 Ne7 13 Qc7 Bxc3† 14 bxc3 Qc6 15 Qxe5 1 - 0 Borisenko - Grechkin, correspondence 1956-7.

5	a4	Bb7
6	axb5	axb5
7	Rxa8	Bxa8
8	Nc3!	

Diagram 8   After 8 Nc3

And now: D1 8...e6; D2 8...c6

D1

8	.....	e6

Given "?!" by Lputjan; it is quite complicated, however.

9	Nxb5	Bxe4
10	Bxc4	Bxf3?!

This natural move runs into trouble. In view of Black's development and White's idea of Bf4, the only other move worth considering is 10...c6, when Lputjan gives 11 Ne5!

Diagram 9   After 11 Ne5

At this point 11...cxb5 12 Bxb5† Ke7 13 Qa4 ± (Lputjan) is insufficient, and 11...f6!? 12 Nc3! fxe5 (12...Bb4 13 Nf3 ±) 13 Nxe4 Qxd4 14 Qe2 (! Or 14 Qh5† g6 15 Qe2; also 14 Qxd4 exd4 15 Bxe6 is ±) 14...Bb4† 15 Kf1 gives Black serious problems, e.g. 15...Nf6 16 Ng5 ± or 15...Be7 16 f3 △ Be3.

A third try, Lputjan's 11...Nf6 12 0-0 Be7 13 Nc3 Bd5 14 Nxd5 Nxd5

15 Bd3 ± is promising only for White, so perhaps the most important line would be 11...Bxg2!?. Then a probable continuation is 12 Rg1 Bd5 13 Bxd5 exd5 (13...cxd5 14 Qa4!) 14 Nc3!? (14 Qe2!? and 14 Qh5 g6 15 Qe2 Be7 16 Qf3!? can also be investigated) 14...Qa5!? (14...Nf6 15 Qa4, e.g. 15...Qb6 16 Qa8? 14...Qh4 15 Bg5 Qxh2 16 Qg4) 15 Qb3 Qa7 16 Bf4 with too much attack.

11	Qxf3	c6
12	0-0!	Qb6

12...cxb5 13 Bxb5† Nd7 14 Bf4 Nf6 15 Ra1 Nd5 16 Ra7 ±± (Lputjan).

13	Nc3	Qxd4
14	Qg3!	Nd7

On 14...Bd6, 15 Be3! Bxg3 16 Bxd4 e5 17 Ba7 picks up a piece.

15	Rd1!	

With the idea 15...Qxc4 16 Qc7 Ngf6 17 Qc8† Ke7 18 Bg5 ±± (Lputjan). Therefore, in Lputjan - Kajdonov, Irkutsk 1983, Black resorted to 15...Qe5, but 16 Bf4 Qa5 17 Bc7 Qa7 18 Ne4 was overwhelming: 18...Ngf6 19 Nd6† Bxd6 20 Qxd6 g6 (20...Nd5 21 Qxc6! Qxc7 22 Bxd5 ±±) 21 b4 Qa4 22 Re1 Nd5 23 Bxd5 cxd5 24 h4 d4 25 Ba5 Qb3 26 Rc1 1 - 0.

The only possibility of saving 8...e6 seems to reside with 10...c6 instead of 10...Bxf3, but for now that doesn't seem worth it.

D2

	8	c6

Diagram 10

After 8...c6

This move has been considered good for Black, partially because of 9 Bf4 e6 10 Be2 Nf6 11 0-0 Be7 ∓ of Bronstein - Simagin, USSR 1983, and 9 e5!? e6 10 Be2(?) h6 11 0-0 Ne7 12 b3 Nd5 Vladimirov - Gusev, USSR 1955, and here 13 Qc2 Bb4 14 Na2 cxb3 15 Qxb3 Be7 16 Ba3 0-0 17 Bxe7 Qxe7 18 Nd2 "=/unclear" is given by ECO, but 18...c5! looks better for Black.

Nevertheless, 9 e5 e6 10 Bg5! has more point, to transfer pieces to the a-file. Then 10...Qc7 11 Qa1 or 10...Qa5 11 Be2 h6 12 Be3 Ne7 13 0-0 Nd5 14 Qa1! might follow; in general, 10 Bg5 seems unclear. We will follow instead a move given by Lputjan:

9	Bg5(!)	Nf6
10	Qa1!?	

Here Lputjan gives 10 e5 Nd5 11 Qa1, but it doesn't seem necessary to commit the e-pawn as yet.

10	.....	Nbd7!

13

10...Bb7 11 Qa7 Qc8 (11...Qc7 12 g3!?) 12 Be2!? and Black is tied up (12...b4? 13 Na4 Nxe4 14 Nb6 Qc7 15 Bf4! Qxf4 16 Qxb7 Qd6 17 Bxc4 e6 18 Ne5 Be7 19 Nc8 etc.).

| 11 e5 | Nd5 |
| 12 Ne4 | |

Threatening 13 Nd6†.

12	Qb8
13 e6!	fxe6
14 Be2	

Diagram 11   After 14 Be2

Of course both sides have options, but this is a fairly forcing sequence. Now White would like to play Bh4-g3 and/or 0-0, e.g. certainly 14...g6? 15 Bh4 Bg7 16 Bg3 is too slow: 16...Qc8 17 Neg5 Nf8 18 Ne5 etc.. Possibly 14...h6 15 Bh4 g5 16 Bg3 Nf4 is best, yet 17 h4! keeps the pressure on, or perhaps even 17 Nfxg5!? hxg5 18 Nxg5 with unclear complications.

As a whole, 3 Nf3 a6 4 e4 offers White plenty of play, with advantage in most lines.

II 3 Nf3 Nf6 4 Nc3: Odd Fourth Moves

1	d4	d5
2	c4	dxc4
3	Nf3	Nf6
4	Nc3	

Diagram 12   After 4 Nc3

4 Nc3 is the most active approach to the Queen's Gambit Accepted at White's disposal. By pushing ahead with e4 and/or d5, he secures a complex middlegame and reduces the likelihood of a draw. On the dark side, the knight move does nothing towards recovering the lost c-pawn, which Black can now attempt to hold via 4...a6 or 4...c6 (both intending ...b5). If White then plays 5 e4(!), he is committed to gambit play against an opponent with no apparent weaknesses. It turns out, however, that development and space count for a lot, and no one has discovered a satisfactory antidote to the main lines. In this chapter, we take a look at less ambitious fourth moves by Black, with which he renounces material gain and tries to achieve a balanced middle-game. With the increasing success of White's gambit play, particularly after 4...a6 5 e4, the line 4...c5 has recently come to the forefront, and may be considered the most important of the options below.

We examine, in turn: A 4...Bf5; B 4...e6; C 4...c5.

Other moves aren't seen much:

(a) 4...Nbd7 5 e4 Nb6 6 a4 a5 7 Ne5 e6 (7...c5 8 d5 e6 9 Nxc4 △ 9... Nxc4 10 Bxc4 exd5 11 Nxd5 Be6?! 12 Nxf6† ±, or 9...exd5 10 Nxb6 Qxb6 11 Bb5† Bd7 12 Nxd5 etc.) 8 Nxc4 c6 (8...Bb4 9 Nxb6 cxb6 10 Bb5† Bd7 11 Qe2) 9 Bd3! Najdorf - Reshevsky, Buenos Aires 1953; "±" ECO;

(b) Rare by this order but playable is 4...Nc6 with a Chigorin's Defense to the Queen's Gambit. This is one of White's better lines, and he has no shortage of attacking ideas. As I pointed out in a recent article, the move 5 Bg5 is giving Black difficulties, △ 5...Nd5 6 e4 ±, 5...Bg4 6 e3 (or 6 d5!?), or 5...h6 6 Bh4 e6 7 e3!. Also, the simple 5 e3 Bg4 6 Bxc4 e6 7 h3 (7Bb5!?) 7...Bh5 (or 7... Bxf3!? 8 Qxf3 and White has the two bishops) 8 Bb5! is an option not avail-able to White in the main 4 e3 Bg4 Q.G.A., e.g. 8...Bd6 (8...Bb4? 9 g4 Bg6 10 Ne5 Qd5 11 Bxc6† bxc6 12 0-0 ± -- Keene) 9 e4 Bb4 10 Qa4 Bxf3? (10...0-0!?) 11 Bxc6† bxc6 12 Qxc6† Ke7 13 gxf3 Qxd4 14 Qxc7† Nd7 15 Bg5† f6 16 Rd1! and White came out two pawns to the good, Keene - Cox London 1983.

A

4	Bf5
5 e3	e6

5...Bd3?! 6 Bxd3 cxd3 7 Qxd3 Nbd7 (7...c5 8 Qb5†) 8 0-0 c5 9 d5 ±.

6 Bxc4	Nbd7

Here 6...c5 7 Qb3! looks awkward; Black doesn't have ...Bxf3 as he would have had in a line with ...Bg4.

7 0-0	c6

7...c5 8 d5! ±. 7...Be7 8 Re1 0-0 9 e4 ± (ECO); here 8...Ne4 is better, but either 9 Bd3 or 9 Nd2 Nxd2 10 Qxd2! keeps White's advantage.

Diagram 13   After 7...c6

8 Re1

Aside from the text, these moves are instructive:

(a) 8 Qe2(!) may be best. Simic - Skembris, Vrnjacka Banja 1982 saw 8...Nb6 9 Bb3 Ne4 10 Nd2! Nxd2 11 Bxd2 Bg6 12 f4! Be7 13 e4! with advantage, in view of 13...Qxd4† 14 Be3 Qf6 15 f5! etc., or 13...Qd7 14 Be3 (or even 14 d5!?, as played in the game). Again, space was the key to White's advantage;

(b) Also good seems 8 Nh4 Bg4 9 f3 Bh5 10 g4 Bg6 11 Nxg6 hxg6 12 e4 Qb6 13 Rf2 0-0-0 14 Be3 e5 Knaak - Dobrovsky, Trnava 1983, although White's 15 Na4 Qa5 16 Qc2 exd4 17 Bxd4 Ne5 18 Bc3 Qc7 was unclear. Better seems just 15 Rc1(!) △ 16 Qd2 or 16 Na4.

8	Be7

Or 8...Ne4 9 Bd3 (9 Nd2!?) 9...Nxc3 (9...Ndf6 10 Qc2 Nxc3 11 Bxf5! exf5 12 bxc3 ±) 10 bxc3 Bxd3 11 Qxd3 ± (ECO). Then an interesting sequence would be 11...Bd6 12 e4 e5 13 Ng5!? △ 13...h6 14 Nh3 intending f4.

9 e4	Bg4
10 Be3	

White is clearly better. Cafferty and Hooper claim that 10...0-0 planning ...e5 gives good equalizing chances, but 11 h3 Bh5 (11...Bxf3 12 Qxf3 e5 13 Rad1 ±) 12 Qe2 e5 (?, baut 13 Rad1 is next) 13 g4 exd4 14 Nxd4 Bg6 15 f4! or even 15 Nf5 refutes that notion.

B

4	e6
5 e4	Bb4

5...c5 6 d5 is 'C' below. But also good is 6 Bxc4 exd4 7 Nxd4 Nbd7

(7...a6 8 e5 Qc7 9 Qe2 ±) 8 0-0 Bc5 (8...Be7? 9 Bxe6!) 9 Nb3 Be7 10 Qe2
e5 11 Be3 ± Hübner - Radulov, Leningrad 1973.

6 Bg5

Diagram 14   After 6 Bg5

This is the Vienna System, which has been out of favor for many years.
The play is complex, however, and White must know what he's doing. First,
Black chooses from: B1 6...h6; B2 6...b5; B3 6...c5.

The Vienna lines are covered very well in ECO, and I should point out that
"ECO" for this 4...e6 material refers to the section done by Gipslis, based in
part on work by Taimanov.

B1

	6	h6
	7 Bxf6	Qxf6
	8 Bxc4	0-0

8...c5 is weakening: 9 e5 Qe7 (9...Qd8 10 0-0 Bxc3 [10...cxd4 11 Ne4!
±] 11 bxc3 cxd4 12 Qxd4!? Nc6 13 Qg4 0-0 14 Rb1 ± ECO) 10 0-0 Bxc3
11 bxc3 0-0, and now ECO gives 12 Qe2 Nc6 13 a3 Rd8 14 Qe4 ±, which
looks very good, whereas Gligoric - Kostic, Yugoslavian Ch 1946 went 12 d5
exd5 13 Bxd5 Nd7 14 Rc1 Nb6 15 Be4 "±" ECO.

	9 0-0	Nd7
	10 e5!	Qd8
	11 Qe2	Nb6
	12 Bd3	Nd5
	13 Bc2	

Diagram 15   After 13 Bc2

All natural and good for White. In Averkin - Nikolic, Sochi 1983, Black

17

was reduced to 13...c5 (otherwise the attack is too strong) 14 Nxd5! exd5 (14...Qxd5 15 a3 Ba5 16 Be4 and 17 dxc5) 15 a3 Ba5 16 dxc5 Bc7 17 Nd4! Qe7 18 Qd3 g6 19 Rae1 Qxc5 20 e6 Qd6 21 g3 Bb6 22 Nf5! gxf5 23 Qxf5 Kg7 24 Qh7† Kf6 25 Qxh6† Ke7 26 Qg5† Ke8 27 Ba4† 1 - 0. 6...h6 is too passive.

B2

| | 6 ..... | b5 |

The most popular move in the few games of the 80's, as Black has lost faith in 6...c5. But now the first player exploits his big lead in development.

7 a4(!)

White can demonstrate a safe advantage now. Actually, although the previously-favored 7 e5 h6 8 Bh4 g5 9 Nxg5 hxg5 10 Bxg5 Nbd7 is now considered somewhat unclear, it probably also leads to advantage.

	7	c6
	8 e5	h6
	9 exf6	

A simplifying approach, by which White decimates the Black kingside.

	9	hxg5
	10 fxg7	Rg8
	11 h4!	

Diagram 16   After 11 h4

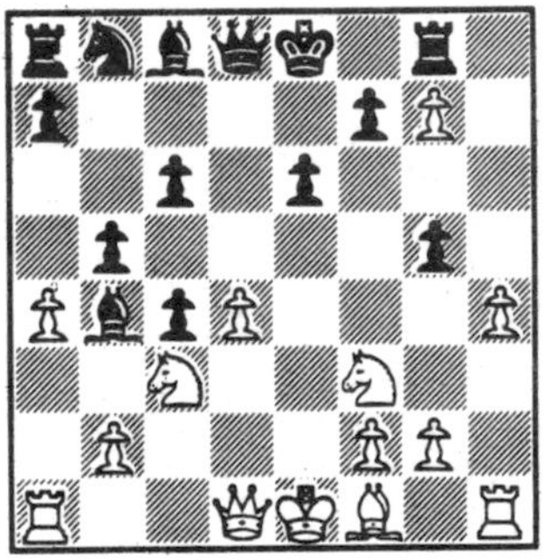

Opening lines. 11 g3 Nd7 (11...g4 12 Nh4!; 11...Bb7 12 Bg2 c5!?) 12 Bg2 Bb7 13 h4 gxh4 14 Rxh4 Qf6 15 Kf1! of Popov - Schmidt, Varna 1967 ("±" ECO) is also promising.

| | 11 ..... | Rxg7 |

Probably best. "11...gxh4 12 Rxh4 ±" (Panchenko) is apparently based upon 12...Qf6 13 g3! intending Bg2 and Ne5 (with Rf4 in some cases), or 13 Qe2!? △Qe4. But 11...g4!? has its risks too due to 12 h5! (or 12 Ng5 -- Panchenko; or 12 Ne5 Rxg7 13 h5), which has won two nice games after 12...Rxg7 (12...gxf3?? 13 h6):

(a) 13 h6 Rh7 14 Ne5 f5 15 Rh5 Bb7 16 Nxg4! fxg4 17 Qxg4 Kd7 18 axb5 Kc7 19 Bxc4 ± / ± Knaak - Bernard, Rostock 1984;

(b) 13 Ne5 f5 14 Be2!? Qd5!? 15 Kf1 Bxc3 16 bxc3 Nd7 17 h6 Rh7 18 Qc2! Nxe5 19 dxe5 Bb7 20 Rd1 Qxe5 21 Bxg4 c5!? 22 axb5 Be4 23 Bh5† with an ongoing attack based upon the open file and Black's dark-squared problems, Tukmakov - Kupreichik, Erevan 1982.

12 hxg5

12 Nxg5 Bb7 "unclear" (Panchenko); the text is more logical.

| | 12 ..... | Nd7 |

12...Rg8? 13 Ne5! intending axb5 and Qf3.

| | 13 Rh8† | Nf8 |
| | 14 Ne5 | |

Panchenko gives 14 g3, and since 14...Bb7 15 Bg2 c5 16 dxc5 is not a serious problem, this may be a good idea.

| | 14 ..... | Bb7 |

This is Vaiser - Panchenko, Sochi 1982, where White played the natural 15 Qf3?! Qxd4 16 Nxc6, but got nothing special after 16...Bxc3† (or 16...Qc5 =) 17 bxc3 Qc5 18 axb5 Qxb5 19 Qf6 Qxg5 =. However, by 15 f4(!), White establishes his command of the center and threatens 16 Ng4 (16...Be7 17 Ne4) as well as e.g. Be2-f3 with axb5. Black could try 15...Qa5, but then 16 axb5 Bxc3† 17 Kf2 Qxb5 18 bxc3 Qb2† 19 Be2 leaves too many weaknesses.

Thus the whole defense with 6...b5 appears a bad bargain for the second player.

B3

| | 6 ..... | c5 |

The old main line of the Vienna System. Now the play after 7 e5 cxd4 is extraordinarily complex, although it is considered ultimately in White's favor. But there are some untried suggestions which might challenge that, and most experienced grandmasters prefer to sidestep this whole problem by another effective sequence:

| | 7 Bxc4 | cxd4 |

The immediate 7...Qa5 8 Bxf6 Bxc3† 9 bxc3 Qxc3† allows 10 Nd2 gxf6 11 dxc5! Ke7 (11...Nd7 12 0-0 Nxc5 13 Rc1 Qd4 14 Qh5! ± ECO) 12 Rc1 Christoffel - Burghold, Montreux 1939; "±" (ECO).

| | 8 Nxd4 | |

Diagram 17   After 8 Nxd4

| | 8 ..... | Qa5 |

The most critical move, although perhaps not best. Others:

(a) 8...Nbd7 9 0-0 Bxc3 (9...h6 10 Bh4 g5 11 Bg3 Bxc3 12 bxc3 Nxe4 13 Bxe6! ± ECO) 10 bxc3 Qa5 11 Bxf6 Nxf6 12 Bb5†! Nd7 (12...Bd7 13 e5 Bxb5 14 Nxb5 Qxb5 15 exf6 gxf6 16 Qf3 ± ECO) 13 Qg4 0-0 14 Nxe6! fxe6 15 Qxe6† Rf7 16 Bc4 Qh5 17 Rad1 Nf8 18 Qe7! ± Trifunovic - Karaklaic, Yugoslavian Ch 1951; the Black bishop on c8 can't find its way out, e.g.

18...b5 19 Bb3 Ba6 20 Rd6 etc..

(b) 8...Qc7 9 Qb3! Qc5 (9...Bxc3† 10 Qxc3! Nxe4 11 Nb5! Qc5 12 Qxg7 Rf8 13 Bh6! Qxf2† 14 Kd1 Nd7 15 Re1 Nef6 16 Bxe6! Qxb2 17 Rc1 1-0 Averbach - Estrin, Moscow 1964; 9...Nxe4 10 Qxb4 Nxg5 11 0-0 ± ECO; actually, 11 h4! Qe5† 12 Nde2 Nc6 13 Qb5 wins a piece) 10 Bxf6 gxf6 11 0-0 Qxd4 12 Qxb4 Nc6 13 Qb3 0-0 14 Rad1 ± (ECO).

(c) 8...Bxc3† 9 bxc3 h6(!) will favor White, but at least Black survives with minimal damage in the line 10 Bxf6 Qxf6 11 0-0 0-0 12 f4! Bd7 13 e5 Qe7 14 Rb1! ± △ Qg4 (ECO). White's 14th replaces the careless 14 Rf3? Nc6 15 Nb3 Rad8 16 Rg3 f6 = Pirc - Karklaic, Belgrade 1952. Since 14 Rb1 Bc6(?) 15 f5! exf5 16 e6 is terrific for White, 14...Qc5 looks forced, when 15 Bb3(!) Qxc3 16 Kh1 yields an interesting White attack.

Perhaps this line really didn't catch on due to 10 Bh4!?, e.g. 10...g5 11 Bg3 Nxe4 12 Be5!?, but in that case 12...f6(!) seems surprisingly safe (13 Qh5† Ke7), so I would recommend 10 Bxf6.

9 Bxf6	Bxc3†

9...gxf6 more or less wastes ...Qa5: 10 0-0 Bxc3 (10...Bd7? 11 Rc1 Nc6 12 a3! Bxc3 13 Rxc3 Qe5 14 Nb5! Ke7 15 f4 Qb8 16 Rd3 Rd8 17 Qh5 ± Podgorny - Barcza, Karlovy Vary 1948) 11 bxc3 Nd7 (11...Qxc3? 12 Rc1 and 13 Bb5† is too strong) 12 Kh1 (!? 12 Nb5, or even 12 f4!? Qxc3 13 Nb5! Qe3† 14 Kh1) 12...Nb6? (12...a6 ECO), although 13 f4! looks good) 13 Bb5† (or 13 Bb3 Bd7 14 Qf3 ± Kotov - Yudovich, USSR Ch 1939) 13...Bd7 14 Qh5! Bxb5 15 Nxb5 0-0 16 f4 Kh8 17 Qh6! ± (ECO).

10 bxc3	Qxc3†
11 Kf1	

Diagram 18   After 11 Kf1

11	Qxc4†

11...gxf6? 12 Rc1 Qa5 is dubious after both 13 Nb5 Na6 (13...0-0? 14 Rc3) 14 Qd4 Ke7 15 Qd6† Ke8 16 e5! ± (Judovic) or 13 Bb5† Ke7 14 e5! fxe5 15 Qh5! intending 15...f6 16 Bc4! Nc6 17 Nf5† ±±, or here 15...exd4 16 Qg5† or 15...Qd2 16 Nb3 Qf4 17 g3! ±± (various).

12 Kg1	Nd7

Obviously not 12...gxf6? 13 Rc1, but 12...Bd7? 13 Rc1 is also bad: 13...Qa6 14 Nxe6! fxe6 (14...Qxe6 15 Rc8†!) 15 Rc8†! ±± Alekhine et al. - Bogoljubov et al., Warsaw 1941.

Finally, 12...0-0? loses to 13 Qg4 g6 14 Qf4 (14 e5! Samarian, although 14...h5! and 15...Kh7 holds on) 14...Nd7 15 e5 Nxf6 16 exf6 Kh8 17 Rc1

2d5 18 Qh6 Rg8 19 Nf3 Qh5 20 Ng5! ⩲ (Kotov).

13 Rc1

Diagram 19   After 13 Rc1

13 .....   Qa6

(a) 13...Qxa2? 14 Bxg7 Rg8 15 Nb5 ±;

(b) 13...Qb4? is bad, as was demonstrated in Ermolinsky - Speelman, Lenin-
grad 1984: 14 Bxg7 Rg8 15 Nxe6! fxe6 16 Qh5† Kd8 17 Qxh7 Rxg7 18
Qxg7 Qd2 (Black can't wait around for h4-h5-h6 etc.) 19 Qc3 Qxc3 20
Rxc3 Nf6 21 f3 and the kingside pawns are too strong.

14 Bxg7   Rg8
15 Bh6

Here Samarian awards 15 a4 an "!" and calls it a "very important improvement", but then his analysis shows 15 a4 leading to very little versus proper
play, and 15 Bh6 leading to a clear White advantage! In fact, after 15 Bh6
Black faces some rather sad options:

(a) 15...e5 16 Nf5 Qg6 17 Nd6† Ke7 18 Nf5† Ke8 Maderna - Euwe, Mar
del Plata 1944, and now 19 g3! △ Rc7 is strong (19...Nf6 20 Nd6† Ke7 21
Rc7†) -- various;

(b) 15...Nf6 16 e5 Nd5 17 h4! Bd7 18 Qc2 Rg6 19 h5! ± Stahlberg - Sefe,
Toplice 1949 (19...Rxh6 20 Qd2);

(c) 15...Ne5 16 Qh5! Qa5 (16...Nd3 17 Nb5!) 17 Bf4 Nc4 18 Qxh7 Rg4
19 Qh8† Ke7 20 Bh6 e5 21 Bf8† Kd7 22 Nb3 Qxa2 23 Qf6! 1 - 0, intending 23...Qxb3 24 Qxf7†, Maderna - Szabo, Mar del Plata 1948.

Thus one can see that 4...e6 and transposition to the Vienna System is
wholly unappealing for Black if White knows his stuff. This brings us to the
most frequent option to 4...a6 and 4...c6:

C

4 .....   c5

(See the diagram on the next page)

With this move Black introduces a direct strategy of destroying White's
central pawns. This deserves close attention; after 5 d5 e6, many complicated
ideas are still unexplored, as may be seen in the sidelines which follow.

5 d5

As it stands, 5 e4!? promises to be a good alternative, △ 5...e6 6 Bxc4
xd4 7 Nxd4, e.g. 7...Nbd7 8 0-0 Bc5 9 Nb3 ±; or 5...cxd4 6 Qxd4!

Diagram 20 — After 4...c5

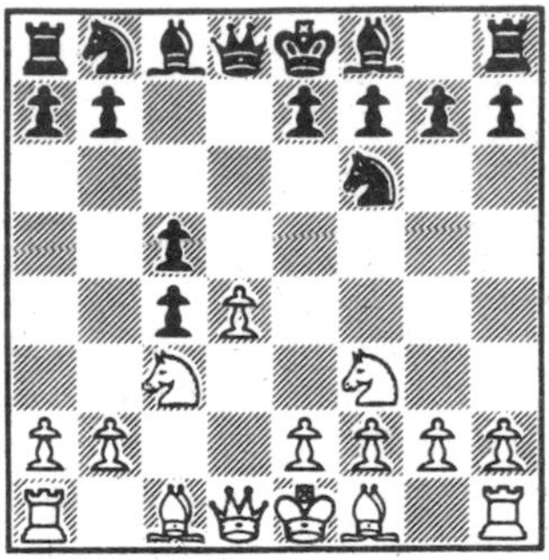

(6 Nxd4 e5!? 7 Ndb5 Be6 looks better than ECO's 6...a6) 6...Qxd4 7 Nxd4, which also seems to favor White, e.g. 7...e5 8 Ndb5 Na6 9 Bxc4 ± (ECO). Perhaps 5 e4 b5!? is possible, intending 6 e5 Nd5 7 Nxb5 Qa5† or 6 Nxb5 Qa5† 7 Nc3 Nxe4, but of course this is loosening. 5 d5 is more assertive, cramping Black's game in order to force a confrontation.

5 .....   **e6**

5...Bf5 6 Ne5 (6 Nh4(!) looks a good alternative, to enforce e4; ECO gives another idea, 6 Qa4† Nbd7 7 Qxc4 e6 8 dxe6 Bxe6 9 Qa4 h6(?) 10 g3 Puck - Susic, Yugoslavia 1968, but this is not so convincing. Finally, 6 e3!? e6 7 Bxc4 exd5 8 Nxd5 Nc6 9 Qb3 Rb8 led to a quick draw in Gorelov - Suetin, Moscow 1984) 6...a6 (6...e6 can apparently be met by 7 Qa4† Nbd7 8 e4!, e.g. 8...Nxe4 9 Nxe4 Bxe4 10 dxe6 fxe6 11 Bxc4 etc., or 8...Bxe4 9 dxe6 fxe6 10 Nxe4 Nxe4 11 Bxc4 etc.; 6...Nbd7? 7 Nxc4 Nb6 8 e4! ±) 7 Nxc4! (7 a4 e6!) 7...b5 8 Ne3 Bc8 9 g3 Bb7 10 Bg2 (±) 10...Nbd7 11 0-0 g6 (11... Nb6 12 a4! b4 13 a5 bxc3 14 axb6 cxb2 15 Bxb2 Qxb6 16 Nc4 Qb5 17 Qd3 ±) 12 a4! b4 13 Ne4 Nxe4 14 Bxe4 Bg7 (14...a5 15 Bg2 Bg7 16 Nc4) 15 a5 ± (or 15 Bg2 ±) Furman - Suetin, USSR Ch 1965.

6 e4   **exd5**

(a) Now it's too late for 6...b5?! due to 7 Nxb5 Qa5† 8 Nc3 Nxe4 9 Bd2 Nxd2 10 Qxd2 (or even 10 Nxd2!?) 10...Be7 11 Bxc4 Ba6 12 Bxa6 Qxa6 13 0-0-0 ± Shamkovich - Muhin, USSR Ch 1972;

(b) 6...a6!? looks reasonable. Then 7 Bxc4 b5 8 Bb3 is possible, and 7 d6!? should also be considered, e.g. 7...Nc6 8 e5 Ng4 9 Bf4. Perhaps best is 7 Bg5(!) △ 7...h6 8 Bxf6 gxf6 9 Bxc4 ± or 7...Be7? 8 d6! or 7...b5 8 e5 h6 9 Bh4 g5 10 Nxg5! etc.. Tests are needed here.

(c) 6...Nxe4!? 7 Nxe4 exd5 gives Black three pawns for a piece, but Cafferty and Hooper give 8 Ng3 or 8 Bg5 f6 9 Bxf6! gxf6 10 Qxd5 etc.; better 8... Qa5† 9 Bd2 Qd8.

7 e5

(See the diagram on the next page)

7 .....   **Nfd7**

An important decision:

(a) 7...d4 8 Bxc4 Nc6? (8...dxc3!? 9 Bxf7† Ke7 10 exf6† gxf6 seems to improve, but then even 11 Qxd8† and 12 bxc3 is ±) 9 exf6 dxc3 10 Qe2† Kd7 11 Bf4 Qa5 12 Rd1† Nd4 13 Bb5† ±± Uhlmann - Wade, Hastings 1958-9;

Diagram 21

After 7 e5

(b) 7...Ng8? 8 Qxd5 Nc6 9 Bxc4 Be6 10 Qe4 Vladimir - Hodos, USSR 1958. White has development and all the squares, and 10...Nd4!? can be met by 11 Be3! Nxf3† 12 gxf3 ±;

(c) 7...Ne4!? 8 Qxd5! (replacing 8 Nxe4 dxe4 9 Qxd8† Kxd8 10 Ng5 Be6 11 Nxe6† fxe6 12 Bxc4 of Petrosian - Buslayev, USSR 1960, and now 12... Nc6! was unclear -- Gligoric; 8 Nxd5 Be6 9 Bxc4 Qa5† 10 Bd2 Nxd2 11 Qxd2 ± Farago)8...Nxc3 9 Qxd8† Kxd8 10 bxc3 Be6 (10...Bg4 11 Nd2!) 11 Ng5 Nd7 (11...Bd5 12 Be3! △Rd1 -- Gligoric) 12 Nxe6† fxe6 13 f4! Nb6 14 a4 g5 ("!" Gligoric; 14...a5!?) 15 a5! Nd5 16 f5! exf5 17 Bxc4 Nf4 (17... Nxc3? 18 Bb2 Ne4 19 e6) 18 0-0 Be7 19 g3 Ng6 20 Rxf5 Rf8 21 Rxf8 Nxf8 22 Bd5 Rb8 23 c4 and the bishops dominate, Gligoric - Nikolic, Niksic 1983.

A great demonstration of White's play, but also a place for investigation.

8 Bg5!

The two alternatives are less convincing, e.g. 8 Nxd5 Nb6 9 Nxb6 Qxd1† 10 Kxd1 axb6 ½ - ½ Torre - Radulov, Indonesia 1983, or 8 Qxd5 Nb6 (or 8... Nc6!? 9 Bxc4 Ndxe5 unclear -- Petrosian) 9 Qxd8† Kxd8 10 Bg5† Ke8 11 0-0-0 Be7 = of Torre - Seirawan, London 1984.

8 ..... Be7

8...f6!? is supposed to be bad due to 9 ext6 Nxf6(?) 10 Dxf6 gxf6 11 Nxd5 b5 12 Qe2† Kf7 13 0-0-0 ± Korelov - Miezes, USSR 1964. But here 9...gxf6!? strikes me as unclear, since the attacks after 10 Qxd5 Qe7†! and 10 Nxd5 fxg5 11 Bxc4!? Nb6 are at best risky. And, although 10 Bf4 is safer, 10...Nb6! (10...d4? 11 Nd5 ±) 11 Nh4 (11 Ne5 fxe5 12 Qh5† Kd7) 11...Be6 12 Nb5 Na6 13 Be2 d4 14 Bh5† Kd7 15 0-0 is also obscure. Perhaps the alternate piece sacrifice 10 Nxd5 gxf5 11 Qe2†(!) Kf7 12 0-0-0 should be looked into, and 12...Nc6 13 Qe3 or 12...b5 13 h4!.

9 Bxe7   Qxe7
10 Nxd5   Qd8
11 Bxc4   0-0

Played in each of the games with this line, but the alternatives are interesting:

(a) 11...Qa5†? 12 Qd2! Qxd2† 13 Kxd2 looks excellent for White, e.g. 13... Kd8 (13...Nb6 14 Nc7† Kd8 15 Nxa8 Nxc4† 16 Kc3 Na5 17 Rad1† and 18 Ng5) 14 Rhe1 Nc6 (14...h6 15 Kc3 or even 15 e6 fxe6 16 Nf4) 15 Kc3 Re8 16 Rad1 h6 (16...b6 17 Ng5) 17 Nf4 ±± (17...g5 18 Nh5);

(b) 11...Nb6 12 Nxb6 Qxb6 13 0-0 0-0 14 Ng5!? (14 Qc2! ± △ Ng5 or Rd1-d6) 14...h6! 15 Nxf7 (15 Ne4!? Qxb2 16 Nd6 Nc6(!) is unclear) 15...Rxf7 16 Qd5 Qc7 17 Rad1 ("±" *Informant*) 17...Nc6 18 Qxc5 Kh8 Vaiser - Mirkovic, Vrnjacka Banja 1984. Here Vaiser continued 19 Bxf7!? Qxf7 20 b4 Bg4! 21 f3 Be6 22 a3!? Rc8 and Black had survived (½ - ½, 48), although one may want to claim a slight ±. As an alternative, 19 e6!? has its points.

Diagram 22   After 19 e6

Then Black has very little choice, as 19...Qe7 20 Rd6! rook moves 21 Rxc6 gives a winning ending, and 19...Rf6 20 Rfe1! Qe7 21 Qxe7 Nxe7 22 Rd8† and 23 Re8 is also winning. So 19...Re7! 20 Rd6! and Black must play 20...Na5! (20...Qb6 21 Rxc6) 21 Qxc7 Rxc7 22 Bd3 (22 Rd8†!?) with new difficulties, e.g. 23...g6!? 23 Rfe1 Re7 24 Bxg6 Nc4 25 Rd8† Kg7 26 Re8 Kf6 27 Rxe7 Kxe7 28 b3 Nd6 29 f4. The possibilities are practically unlimited here, and White may want to sidestep this whole line by the simpler 14 Qc2.

(c) 11...Nc6 is obvious and yet hasn't to my knowledge been played. Now an idea similar to the text below is 12 Qa4!? 0-0 (12...Qa5† 13 Qxa5 Nxa5 14 Bb5 ±) 13 0-0-0 △ 13...Ndxe5 14 Rfe1.

The other unique response to 11...Nc6 is 12 e6(!) fxe6 13 Nf4 (not available after 11...0-0), and e.g. 13...Qa5† 14 Kf1 or 13...Nb6 14 Bxe6 with a small advantage which endures into the endgame. This also needs tests.

12 Qc2!

Petrosian's move. 12 0-0 is held to be equal (or "feeble" -- Keene, but that is exaggerated). A good illustration was Miles - Seirawan, London 1984: 12...Nc6 13 Re1 Nb6 (or 13...Re8 of Marovic - Radulov, Amsterdam 1973, although White might have tried 14 e6!? or 14 Nf4) 14 Nxb6 axb6 15 Qe2 Qe7 16 a3 (16 Qe4!?) 16...Be6 17 Bxe6 Qxe6 =.

Diagram 23   After 12 Qc2

12 .....   **Re8**

(a) 12...Nc6 13 0-0-0 Re8 14 Rhe1 is just a transposition, or here 13... Ndxe5? 14 Nxe5 Nxe5 15 Rhe1 forces 15...Nc6 (or 15...Ng6) 16 Ne7† Qxe7 17 Rxe7 Nxe7 which is insufficient after 18 Qe4!. Slow moves such as e.g. 13...a6 14 h4! h6 15 Ng5! lose outright, and after 13...b5!? 14 Bxh5, 14...· Nb4? 15 Nxb4 cxb4 16 Qc6, 14...Bb7 15 Qf5, and 14...Nd4 15 Nxd4 cxd4 16 Rxd4 (16...Qa5?? 17 Ne7† and 18 Qxh7†!) all fail to save Black.

(b) Belyavsky gives "12...b5!?". The idea is clearly 13 Bxb5 Nxe5, but now White has 14 Qe4!(△ Ne7† and Qxa8) 14...Nxf3† 15 gxf3. Then 15...Be6 16 0-0-0 Bxd5 is natural, but 17 Rxd5 contains many threats, e.g. 17...Qa5 (? , but 17...Qf6 18 Rhd1 △ Rd6) 18 Bc4 is terribly strong, intending 18...Nc6? 19 Rh5 g6 20 Qxc6, 18...g6 19 Rd6 △20 Qxa8 or 20 Rxg6†, or 18...Na6 19 Rh5 g6 20 Rg1 △20...Kh8 21 Qe5† f6 22 Qe7 etc..

13 0-0-0   **Nxe5**

13...Nc6 14 Rhe1 is given as "±" by Petrosian, and seems at least so, since e.g. 14...a6 15 Nf4! threatens both 16 e6 and 16 Bxf7†.

14 Rhe1   **Nbc6**
15 Nxe5   **Nxe5**

Not 15...Rxe5 16 Rxe5 Nxe5 17 Qe4 Qd6 18 Nc7! Qxc7 19 Qxe5! ⩱ (Petrosian).

16 Bb5!

Diagram 24   After 16 Bb5

White's attack is now absolutely unstoppable:

(a) 16...Bd7 17 Bxd7 Nxd7 18 Rxe8† Qxe8 19 Nc7 ⩱ ;

(b) 16...Bg4 17 Bxe8 Bxd1 18 Rxd1 c4 19 Qf5! Qxe8 20 Nc7 g6 21 Qf6 Nd3† 22 Rxd3 Qc8 23 Re3 1 - 0 (23...Qxc7 24 Re7) Salov - Radulov, Leningrad 1983;

(c) 16...Re6 17 Nf4 Qf6 18 Qd2! g6 19 Qd8† Kg7 20 Nxe6† Bxe6 (20... fxe6 21 Qxf6† and 22 Rd8) 21 Qxa8 Bxa2 22 Qd8 Qf5 23 Bd3 Qf4† 24 Rd2 and White won shortly, Belyavsky - Seirawan, USSR - ROW, London 1984.

1 d4	d5
2 c4	dxc4
3 Nf3	Nf6
4 Nc3	a6

The main line of this book, which can lead to spectacular combinational play. Black intends to hold the c4 pawn, come what may. Now 5 a4 Nc6! is known to be satisfactory for the second player, in view of 6 e4 Bg4! or 6 e3 Bg4 7 Bxc4 e6, with a Modern (4...Bg4) Queen's Gambit Accepted where a4 is a completely wasted tempo. Also, 6 e3 Na5!? 7 Ne5 Be6 is of interest, e.g. 8 e4 c6 9 f4 b5 unclear. Thus White makes it a real gambit:

5 e4	b5
6 e5	Nd5
7 a4!	

Diagram 25   After 7 a4

Rather than 7 Ng5?! Nxc3 8 bxc3 f6!. After 7 a4!, White will attack according to Black's choice of defensive formation in response to the threat on b5. The "main lines" of the gambit are introduced by 7...c6 and 7...Nxc3, to be dealt with in the following chapters. But two less frequent replies are extremely important: A 7...Bb7; B 7...Nb4.

There are also two irregular moves:

(a) 7...Bf5 has been used to get to the line 8 axb5 Nb4, transposing to 7...Nb4. I think that this is an inferior order, however, due to 8 Nh4(!) Nxc3 (forced, to hold b5) 9 bxc3 Be4 10 e6 (or 10 Qg4 Bd5 11 axb5 axb5 12 Rxa8 and 13 e6) 10...Qd5 (what else?) 11 exf7† Kxf7 (11...Qxf7 12 Qg4!) 12 axb5 △ 12...axb5 13 Rxa8 Qxa8 14 Qh5† ±;

(b) 7...b4 (usually given "?") 8 Ne4 is called '±., but now 8...c3! 9 bxc3 bxc3 is not effortlessly favorable for White. For example, 10 Qb3 Nc6 11 Nxc3 Be6! is unclear (although 12 a5 may be lightly ±). Another idea would be 10 Ba3 Bf5 11 Ng3 Bg4 12 Be2, to recover the pawn "at leisure", e.g. 12.. e6 13 Bxf8 Kxf8 14 h3 Bxf3 15 Bxf3, but in any case the d-pawn may come under pressure. Better seems the straightforward 10 Bc4 Bf5 11 Ng3 Bg4 12 h3 Bxf3 13 Qxf3 e6 14 0-0 ±, with plans to use White's space advantage, e.g. 14...Be7 15 Qg4 or 14...Nc6 15 Be3 Qd7 16 Rac1 etc..

A

7	Bb7

This has been the least used of Black's traditional strategies, but it is very unclear and leads to some remarkable positions after:

8 e6!   fxe6

8...f6!? 9 Ne4! (9 Nh4?! Nxc3 10 Qh5† g6 11 Nxg6 Qd5!)

Diagram 26   After 9 Ne4

9...Nb4! (9...Ne3 10 Bxe3 Bxe4 11 Nd2! Bd5 12 axb5 axb5 13 Rxa8 Bxa8 14 Qh5† g6 15 Qxb5† ± Vaiser - Romanishin, USSR 1973) 10 Nc5! Bxf3 11 gxf3 N8c6 (11...Qxd4 12 Qxd4 Nc2† 13 Kd1 Nxd4 14 Be3 ±; compare note ,(a)' to the next diagram) 12 Be3 Nxd4 13 Bxd4 Qxd4 14 Qxd4 Nc2† Kd2! Nxd4 16 Kc3! Rd8 Chiburdanidze - Sturua, USSR 1982, and here 17 Nxa6! Nxe6 (versus 18 Nxc7 mate) 18 axb5 with the idea 19 Bxc4 was ± (Chiburdanidze).

9 Ne4

Threatening Nc5 and preventing ...Qd7 or ...Qd6. 9 Be2 Nxc3!? 10 bxc3 is analysed under the order 7...Nxc3 8 bxc3 Bb7 9 e6 fxe6 10 Be2 below, but 9...Nxc3 is not forced.

9 Ne5!? might lead to 9...Nxc3 (! 9...Nf6 10 axb5) 10 Qh5† g6 11 Nxg6 hxg6 12 Qxh8 Nd5 13 Bh6 Kf7 14 Qh7† Kf6 =, and 9 Ng5!? is also untested.

9 .....   Nb4

Again 9...Ne3? fails to 10 Bxe3 Bxe4 11 Nd2 Bb7 12 axb5 axb5 13 Rxa8 and 14 Qh5†. Perhaps 9...Nd7!? could be tried, although 10 Neg5 (10 Nfg5 e5(!) 11 Qf3!?) 10...Ndf6 11 Ne5 (11 Nxe6 Qc8 12 Nxf8 Rxf8 13 Be2 unclear) 11...Qc8 12 b3! cxb3 13 axb5 (or perhaps 13 Qxb3 b4 14 a5) 13...axb5 14 Bxb5† c6 15 Rxa8 Qxa8 16 Bc4 gives White a nice game. Here 12 Be2 would be a slower approach, e.g. 12...c5(!) (12...g6 13 h4) 13 0-0 g6 14 axb5 axb5 15 Rxa8 Bxa8 16 Re1 h5 17 Ngf3 etc.; but 12 b3 looks better.

10 Nc5   Bxf3
11 gxf3

(See the diagram on the next page)

Similar to the note to 8...fxe6. Black has two critical moves:

(a) 11...Qxd4 12 Qxd4 Nc2† 13 Kd1 Nxd4 14 Be3. Amazingly, Black's *three* extra pawns may not suffice for equality! Taimanov says "unclear", but I think Black is in some trouble, e.g. 14...N8c6 15 axb5 Nxb5 (15...Rd8 16 dxc6! Nb3† 17 Nd7 Nxa1 18 Bxc4 ± △ Kd2 and Rxa1) 16 Nxe6 or 16 Bxc4 with advantage. Or 14...e5 15 axb5 e6 16 Bxd4! exd4 17 Nxe6 followed by Bxc4. Or 14...Nb3(!) 15 Nxb3 cxb3 16 axb5 a5! 17 Bc4 (17 f4!? Nd7 18

Diagram 27

After 11 gxf3

Bg2 Rd8 unclear) 17...Kf7 18 Bxb3 Nd7 19 Ke2 △ Rhc1 and White still retains the better chances;

(b) 11...N8c6 12 Nxe6! Qd6 13 d5 Qe5† (13...Nxd5 14 Qxd5!) 14 Be3 Gufeld - Kagan, USSR 1964. ECO calls this position "=/ unclear", but let's follow the original game: 14...Nd8 (14...Qxb2 15 Rc1!) 15 axb5

Diagram 28

After 15 axb5

15...Nxe6 (15...Qxb2 16 Nxc7†!!? Kd7 17 Nxa8 Nc2† 18 Qxc2 Qxc2 19 Bh3† Ke8?! 20.Nc7† Kf7 21 bxa6! Qc3† 22 Kf1 Qxa1† 23 Kg2 etc. is a crazy line, but really White should choose just 16 Rc1! Nxe6 17 dxe6 Rd8 18 Qa4!, e.g. 18...axb5 19 Qxb5† c6 20 Bxc4!. An amazing line.) 16 dxe6 Rd8 (16...Qxe6 17 Qa4 Nd3† 18 Bxd3 cxd3 19 bxa6† with a7 to follow) 17 Qa4 Qxb2 (17...Qxb5 18 Bxc4!, e.g. 18...Nd3† 19 Ke2 Qxa4 20 Rxa4 Nxb2 21 Bb3! Rb8 22 Rxa6 etc.) 18 bxa6† c6 19 Rc1 g6 20 Bxc4 1 - 0. 20...Bg7 21 0-0 threatens Rb1 among other things.

Black may have some improvements, but one can see that the White attack is extremely dangerous. After some analysis, I still don't see a really satisfactory way for Black to defend.

B

7 ..... Nb4

(See diagram on the next page)

A relatively new move, which has turned out to be yet another source of crazy complications. Black intends simply ...Bf5 and ...Nc2(†).

8 axb5(!)

28

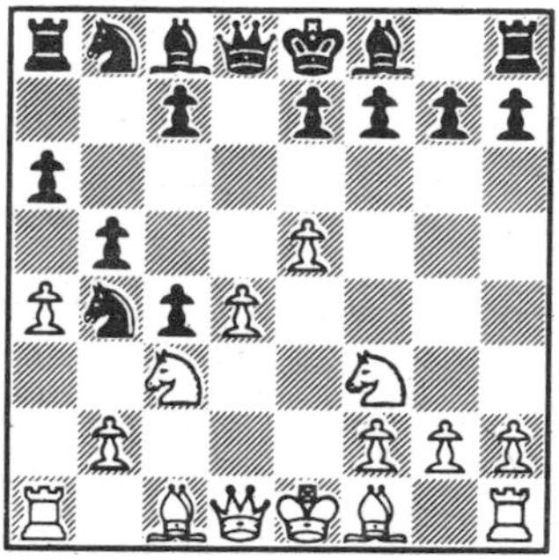

Diagram 29   After 7...Nb4

Also extremely complex, and probably slightly in White's favor, is 8 Be2!? Bf5 9 0-0 Nc2 (else b5 hangs and Black is hopelessly behind in development) 10 Ra2 (10 Rb1!? Nb4 11 Bg5!? Bxb1 12 Qxb1 is given by Knaak, White's 11th to avoid three-fold repetition. Then critical would seem 12...c6 and if 13 e6, 13...f6. Knaak - Donchev, Bratislava 1983 went 10...e6 instead of 10...Nb4, and White got good play following 11 axb5 axb5 12 Nxb5 Nb4 13 Bg5 Qd7 14 Bxc4 Bxb1 15 Qxb1) 10...Nb4 (10...b4? 11 Bxc4 bxc3 12 bxc3 △ 13 Bb3 Nikolic) 11 Ra3 Nc2 (again no choice) 12 Nh4

Diagram 30   After 12 Nh4

12...Bd3 (only move) 13 Bxd3 cxd3 14 e6 fxe6!? (Nikolic gives "14...Nxa3 15 Qf3 fxe6 16 Qxa8 Nc4 17 axb5 axb5 18 Nf3! ±, but Black is two pawns up in this line and there are options, e.g. 16...b4!? 17 Ne4 Nc4 and 18 Nf3 e5!? 19 Nxe5 Nxe5 20 dxe5 e6, although White may well be better in such cases) 15 Qh5† g6 (15...Kd7 16 axb5!? Nxa3 17 bxa3 was Kotronius - Vortruba, Athens 1984, when Black came out about equal following 17...axb5 18 Qxb5† Kc8; 16 Ne4! Nxa3 17 Nc5† Kc8 18 bxa3 Nc6 19 Nxe6 Qd7 Krasenkov - Janovsky, USSR 1985, and now 20 d5! Nd8 21 Ng6 was ± according to Krasenkov; 16 Rb3!? Informant) 16 Nxg6 hxg6 17 Qxh8 b4 18 Bh6 Kd7!? (Nikolic gives 18...bxc3 19 Qxf8† Kd7 20 Qf3 "!", but this is not so clear after 20...c6) 19 Rb3 bxc3, and now instead of 20 bxc3(?) Nc6 21 Rd1 Na5 22 Rbb1 Na3 23 Ra1 N3c4, when Black may be even a bit better, Nikolic suggests 20 Bxf8!? Nc6 21 d5! exd5 22 Qh3† e6 23 Bg7 N2d4 24 Rxc3 Ne2† 25 Kh1 Nxc3 26 Bxc3 "±", and indeed, ± may be the right assessment for this whole line. In Petursson - Thorsteins, Reykjavik 1985, White replaced 19 Rb3 with 19 Bxf8!? bxa3 20 d5 Kc8 21 Qg7, and here Informant suggests

21...a2 22 Bxe7 Qd7 23 Nxa2 exd5 "∞".

8	.....	**Bf5**
9	**Bxc4**	**Nc2†**
10	**Kf1**	**Nxa1**

Yet another great position for analysis. White has a huge lead in development for the rook, and hopes of winning one of Black's loose pieces.

11 g4!?

I like the looks of 11 Ng5(!), which is untried by extremely interesting: 11...e6 12 Qf3! (12 Qa4? Nd7! 13 bxa6 Be7)

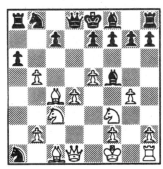

Diagram 31   After 12 Qf3

Now 12...Qxd4? 13 Qxa8 Qxc4† 14 Kg1 is bad, and 12...Ra7 13 d5! (△ 14 Nxf7 or 14 Be3) 13...c5! 14 bxc6 △ 15 Be3 or 15 g4 is at least very difficult for Black. A critical line would be 12...c6(!) 13 bxc6! (13 Nxf7 Qxd4!) 13...Qxd4?! (not best, but it leads to a fun example; 13...Qc7 14 d5 could be looked at) 14 Be2! (14 b3 Ra7!) 14...Qa7 15 c7! Nd7 16 Be3 Bc5 17 Bxc5 Nxc5 18 Qc6† Ke7 (versus 19 c8(Q)†) 19 Nb5! and White wins, in view of 19...axb5 20 Qd6† Ke8 21 Bxb5† etc..

It is in fact possible that 11 Ng5 is the best move, although Kouatly in *Informant* assigns two exclamation points to 11 g4.

Diagram 32   After 11 g4

11 .....   **Bc2!?**

Kouatly gives a convincing line after 11...Be6?: 12 Bxe6 fxe6 13 Ng5 Qd7 14 Qf3 c6 15 Qf7† Kd8 16 Nxe6† Kc8 17 Nxf8 Qxg4 18 Qe8† Kc7 19 Qxe7† Nd7 20 Ne6† Kc8 21 bxc6 ±±, and Padevsky mentions 11...Bg6 12 e6 fxe6 13 Ne5 ±.

But there are two other moves, most notably 11...axb5!? 12 Bxf7† Kxf7

30

13 Ng5† Kg8 14 gxf5 Nc6! 15 Ne6 Qd7 16 Bh6! Nxe5! 17 Rg1 Ng6 18 d5 "unclear" (analysis by Padevsky).

Also, conveniently, nobody mentions 11...Bxg4, when 12 Ng5 Bxd1 draws, but to win it seems 12 Bxf7† Kxf7 13 Ng5† Ke8 14 Qxg4 must be tried, when Black has several candidates including 14...Nb3 and 14...c6!?. White will have to prove that his attack is strong enough in this case to justify choosing 11 g4 over 11 Ng5.

12 Bxf7†	Kxf7
13 Ng5†	Ke8
14 Qf3	Qxd4?

Padevsky gives 14...Ra7! =, and of course White can play for perpetual check by 15 Qf7†. Since 15 d5 Bg6 looks sufficient, 15 Qf7† Kd7 16 Ne6 could follow, but then 16...Qe8 17 Nc5† is drawn again, and here 16 Nce4 Bxe4 17 Nxe4 Nb3! 18 Qxb3 e6!? (18...Qe8 =) risks worse. Again, the value of 11 g4 depends upon a White improvement.

15 Kg2!	axb5

15...c6 16 bxc6 ⩲ (Kouatly).

16 Be3!	Qc4
17 Qxa8	Qc6†

Thus Black got the queens off but was still lost in Kouatly - Radulóv, France - Bulgaria 1984: 18 Qxc6 Nxc6 19 e6?? (19 Rxa1! Nxe5 20 Nxb5 ⩲ Kouatly; not the text, at any rate, which leads to a draw) 19...Nb3 20 Nxb5 g6 21 Nf7 Bg7 22 Nxc7† Kf8 23 Nxh8 Bxh8 24 Bh6† Kg8 25 Re1 Bxb2 26 f3 Bc3!? 27 Re3 Bd2!? 28 Rxb3 Bxb3 29 Bxd2 Nd4 ½ - ½.

On the whole, I like 11 Ng5, but both 11th moves should be studied to assess this new and important line. Should the attack eventually prove less convincing than White would like, the move 8 Be2 also seems to offer the first player a small advantage.

Diagram 44

After 17 Qg4

Errata: This diagram should be on Page 39

IV 4...a6 Gambit With 7...c6

1	d4	d5
2	c4	dxc4
3	Nf3	Nf6
4	Nc3	a6
5	e4	b5
6	e5	Nd5
7	a4	c6

Diagram 33   After 7...c6

This straightforward protection of b5 is the main, and most complicated, variation of the gambit. The variations which follow could constitute a nice booklet on tactics.

8	axb5	Nxc3
9	bxc3	cxb5
10	Ng5!	f6

"!?" (ECO), but it's really quite forced. Cafferty and Hooper give "10... e6 11 Qf3 winning", missing that 11...Ra7 saves everything. Of course 11 Nxf7! does the trick instead. Also bad for Black is 10...Bb7 11 e6, e.g. 11... fxe6 12 Nxe6!? (or 12 Qg4!) 12...Qd7? 13 Qh5† g6 14 Qe5, or here 12... Qd6 13 Qg4 (△ Bf4) 13...Bc8 14 Nxg7† Kd8 15 Qe4 Ra7 16 Bf4 Qb6 17 Be5.

11 Qf3

11 e6!? Qd5! 12 Be2(!!?) was an amazing idea which Pahtz tried out versus Bernard in Rostock 1984. White's compensation for a piece and two pawns (!) after 12...fxg5 13 Bh5† Kd8 (! 13...g6 14 Bf3 Qxe6† 14 Be3! Ra7 15 d5 will snare a rook in a few more moves) is really rather incredible, since now 14 Bf3 Qxe6† 15 Be3 Ra7 16 d5 Qd7 is nothing. Perhaps the whole line was just a miscalculation, but White ended up with very interesting play following 14 0-0 Qxe6 15 Re1 Qf6 (15...Qd7!?) 16 d5 ("∞" *Informant*) 16...Ra7?! (How about 16...g4(!) ?) 17 Be3 Rb7 18 Bd4 Qf5 19 Re5 Qd3 20 Qe1 Nd7 21 Re3 Qf5 22 Bf3 h5?! (22...g4!) 23 d6! exd6 24 Rxa6 Qf7? (24...d5!?) 25 Ra8 Kc7 26 Qa1! d5 27 Qa5† Nb6 28 Bxb6† Rxb6 29 Rxc8† ±.

Well, I don't really believe in this attack, but it says something about the nature of this variation, i.e. that Black's whole structure is deceptively vulnerable.

	11	Ra7

12 e6

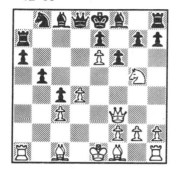

Diagram 34   After 12 e6

This is where the fun really begins! Black has his choice of two wonderful-ly complicated lines: A 12...Qb6; B 12...Bb7.

A

12 .....   Qb6

A later move than 12...Bb7, but perhaps a little easier to deal with. White's next is obviously forced, since e6 is attacked:

13 d5   fxg5

And now we have a further split, this time a choice between two very attractive attacking moves: A1 14 Qf7†; A2 14 Be3.

14 Be3 is given "!" in two *Informants*, but it's not yet established if it is indeed better than 14 Qf7†. 14 Bxg5!? Bxe6 15 Be3 (15 dxe6!? Qxe6† 16 Be2 ∞) 15...Qb7 16 Bxa7!? Bxd5 17 Qe3 e6 18 Bxb8 Qxb8 19 Rxa6 b4, given as unclear by Miles, seems to fall short after 20 Rxe6†!, e.g. 20...Kf7 21 Re5 or 20...Bxe6 21 Qxe6† and 22 Bxc4. But throw in 19...Qc8(!) and Black's probably okay, e.g. 20 Ra2 Bc5 21 Qf4 b4 etc.. Interesting too in this line is 16 dxe6!? Qxf3 17 gxf3 △ f4 and Bg2; still, Black has 17...Rc7! and 18 Bh3 g5! or 18 f4 g6!.

A1

14 Qf7†   Kd8
15 Bxg5

Maybe 15 Be3 Qc7 16 d6!? exd6 17 Bxa7 is worth a look, but that's a lot of pawns to deal with; compare the text.

Diagram 35   After 15 Bxg5

	15	Rd7!!

An astounding idea, and one of the most imaginative moves of modern chess! Black, although under no immediate threat, gives up a whole rook. The point is not just to break the attack but to exploit his only real advantage, the powerful queenside pawns. In fact, 15...Nd7? 16 Rd1! Ne5 17 Qf5 Nd3† 18 Bd3 cxd3 19 Be3 is ± (Miles), and even his suggestion of 15...h6 16 Be3 Qb7 looks insufficient after 17 Bd4! ± (△ Be2-h5 and in some cases Bxg7), or even 17 Be2.

	16 exd7	Nxd7
	17 Be2(?)	h6!
	18 Be3	Qf6!

Already "±", according to Miles.

	19 Qxf6	exf6
	20 Bg4	Bb7
	21 0-0	Bd6

Completing the blockade and consolidating. Sosonko - Rivas, Amsterdam 1978 continued 22 Rfd1 Re8 23 Be6 Nc5 24 Bxc5 Bxc5 25 Bg4 Kc7 and Black proceeded with ...Bd6, ...Kb6, ...a5, and ...b4 with an easily winning game.

While 15...Rd7 is certainly a brilliant try, I think White can improve by (after 16 exd7 Nxd7) 17 Rd1! (△d6), e.g. 17...h6 (17...Ne5 18 Qf4 Ng6 19 d6!!) 18 Be3 Qf6 19 Qe6! Qxc3†!? 20 Bd2 Qe5† (20...Qf6 21 Ba5† Ke8 22 Be2 g6 23 Qc6!) 21 Be2 Kc7! (21...Qc7 22 0-0 Nf6 23 Qe3! △23...Nxd5 24 Ba5!, or otherwise Bc3-e5) 22 Qc6† Kb8 23 g3 g5 24 h4!? Rg8 25 hxg5 hxg5 26 Rh5 (threatens 27 Rxg5 and 28 Bf4, whereas 26...Qf6 allows 27 Bxc4!), and White will be able to play for a win despite the passed pawns. Of course one could analyse forever here, but the whole line looks very difficult for Black.

A2

14 Be3!?

Diagram 36

After 14 Be3

	14	Qc7
	15 Be2!	

With the idea of Qf7† and Bh5 (to answer ...g6 with Bd4), among other ideas. Black has tried two moves after 15 Be2!, neither clearly better than the other:

	15	Nd7!?

15...Rb7 16 g3 ("!" Bohm. Knaak gives 16 0-0 Qe5 17 Qf7† Kd8 18

Bh5 g6(?) 19 Bd4 Qf4 20 Bf3. Thus 16 0-0 may also be good for White. Presumably 16 g3 makes ...Qf4 unavailable in certain variations) 16...Rb6 (16...Bd7 17 0-0 Kd8 18 exd7 Qxd7 19 Bxg5 ± Bohm) 17 h4 g4!? 18 Qf7† Kd8 19 h5! h6 20 0-0-0 Bb7 21 Bxb6 Qxb6 22 Bxg4 and Black was completely paralysed in Langeweg - R. Witt, Dutch Ch 1982.

16	Qf7†	Kd8
17	exd7	Bxd7
18	0-0	

Diagram 37   After 18 0-0

18	.....	Ra8

On the immediate 18...a5, 19 d6! exd6 20 Bxg5† Kc8 21 Bg4! Bxg4 22 Qe8† Kb7 23 Qxb5† (±) seems to be effective, e.g. 23...Ka8 24 Qe8† Qb8 25 Qe4† and 26 Qxg4 or 23...Qb6 24 Qd5† Qc6 25 Rfb1† Kc7 26 Qd4! etc..

19	Bf3	Qd6
20	Bxg5	h6

20...a5 21 Rfe1! △ Re6! is very hard to meet.

21	Be3	a5

21...Qf6 22 Qxf6 exf6 23 d6 (Knaak).

22	Bd4!	Ra6
23	Bh5!	

Threatening Re1-e6. Knaak - Thormann, DDR 1980 continued 23...e5 24 dxe6 Qxe6 25 Qf3! Bc6 26 Qg3 Bd6 27 f4 Rg8 28 Rad1 Kc7 29 Be5! and White was winning, as Black could not cope with the open lines against his king.

One could still debate here, and yet Black can hardly be happy with his practical chances following 12...Qb6.

B

12	.....	Bb7

(See diagram on the next page)

13	Qf4

13 Qf5? Qd5!; the text keeps an eye on b8. But in Vaiser - Vera, East Berlin 1982, White tried a very important new move in a position where none seemed possible: 13 d5!!?

(See diagram on the next page)

Diagram 38   After 12...Bb7

Diagram 39   After 13 d5

Vera played 13...Qxd5 (! 13...Bxd5 14 Qe3 Nc6 [14...fxg5!?] 15 Nf7 Qc8 16 Nxh8 Qxe6 17 Qxe6 Bxe6 18 Be3 Ra8 19 h4! -- Vaiser. Black must then remain a rook down due to the threat of h5-h6 and Ng6, with f4 if necessary; Black's queenside pawns look dangerous, but are difficult to mobilize) 14 Qxd5 Bxd5 15 Be3, and now instead of 15...Rb7? 16 0-0-0! "±" (compare the next note in the main text line; here Black hasn't even ...g6 in), Vaiser recommends 16...fxg5 17 Bxa7 Nc6 18 Rxa6 Nxa7 19 Rxa7 Bxe6 "±". White is quite a bit better, however, after just 20 Be2 (△ Rb7) 20...Bd5! 21 Bf3 Bxf3 (21...e6 22 0-0!) 22 gxf3 g6 23 Kd2 Bg7 (23...Kf7 24 Re1) 24 Ra8 etc..

For now, then, 13 d5 looks quite good, but one example isn't much to go by, and the text (13 Qf4) also seems to give some advantage to White, albeit in an even more complicated way (see the next note):

              13 .....   Qd6(!)

There's little experience with this, but in my opinion the more popular 13...Qc8 (hoping for 14 Nf7 Rg8! or 14 Be3 Bd5 15 Qf5 Qc6 16 Nxh7 Kd8! ∓ Polugayevsky - Gurgenidze, USSR Ch 1967) is simply insufficient after 14 d5! (Zaitsev's recommendation, although I don't believe he analyses it). Play should then go 14...Bxd5 15 Be3! (15 Qd4 is less clear for several reasons. A game Farago - Milanovic, Tuzla 1981 went 15...Qb7 16 Be3 fxg5 17 Qxa7 Qxa7 18 Bxa7 Nc6 19 Rxa6 g6 with complications; here 16...Ra8!? is also obscure, e.g. 17 Rd1? fxg5 18 Qxd5 Qxd5 19 Rxd5 Nc6! or 17 Nf7 Bxe6 18 Nxh8 g6) 15...Rb7 (15...Ra8 16 Qf5 Qc6 17 0-0-0 g6 18 Qxd5 Qxd5 19 Rxd5 fxg5 20 Rc5 is resignable) 16 Qf5

                    (See diagram on the next page)

Diagram 40   After 16 Qf5

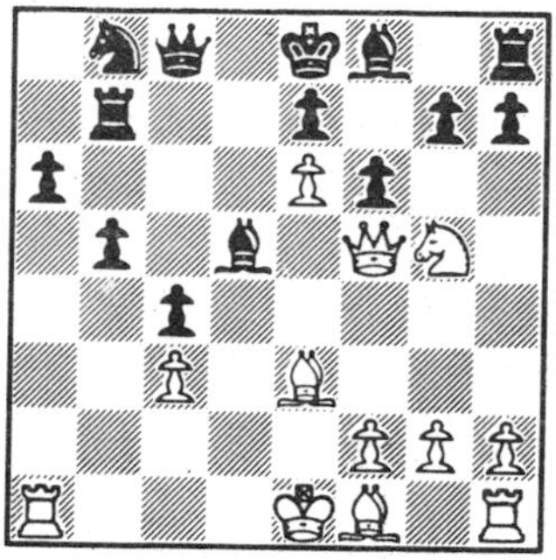

16...Qc6 (16...g6 17 Qxd5 fxg5 18 Qf3!; 16...fxg5 17 Qxd5 Nc6 18 Rxa6 Nd8 19 Be2 Rb8 20 0-0 etc.) 17 0-0-0 g6 18 Qxd5 Qxd5 19 Rxd5 fxg5 20 Rc5! Kd8 21 Be2! with too much attack, e.g. 21...Rc7!? 22 Rd1† Kc8 23 Rxc7† Kxc7 24 Bd4 Rg8 25 Be5† Kc8 26 Rd5! Bg7 27 Rc5† Kb7 28 Bxg7 Rxg7 29 Bf3† ±±. As a Q.G.A. player with Black, I analysed 14 d5! in detail a few years back (with the help of Evan Michaelides), and was so impressed that I first began to take interest in the *White* side of 4 Nc3 a6 5 e4.

14	Nf7!	Qxe6†
15	Be3	Kxf7
16	Qxb8	Qb6
17	d5	Ra8

Diagram 41   After 17...Ra8

Kuzmin - Grigorian, Moscow 1965. White tried 18 Qxa8 Qxe3† 19 fxe3 Bxa8 and Neistadt calls Black better, which may be true after e.g. 20 Rxa6 Bxd5 21 Rb6 e6 22 Rxb5 Bd6 23 e4 Bxe4 24 Bxc4 Bxg2 etc.. The right move, as he points out, is 18 Qxf8†! Rhxf8 19 Bxb6 Bxd5, and now 20 Ba5! (versus 20...a5!) looks correct, with a small edge due to the queenside blockade. Black should move quickly to mobilize his pawns on the other wing, e.g. 20...e5 21 f3 f5 22 Be2 Rg8 or 22...h5!?, but the piece is of greater value, I believe (one idea for White is Rd1-d2, Bd1-c2), and in general 7...c6 looks to be in White's favor. The new move 13 d5!!? also presents difficulties for Black. As a result, tries such as 7...Nb4 or 7...Nxc3 have been replacing 7...c6 as the main way of meeting the gambit.

V 4...a6 Gambit With 7...Nxc3

1	d4	d5
2	c4	dxc4
3	Nf3	Nf6
4	Nc3	a6
5	e4	b5
6	e5	Nd5
7	a4	Nxc3
8	bxc3	

Diagram 42

After 8 bxc3

This position has attracted renewed interest of late, in part because the alternatives have been rather disappointing for Black. After 7...Nxc3, the emphasis is on immediate light-squared control of the center, with ideas such as ...Bb7, ...Be6-d5, and ...Qd5. White is naturally glad to have his center strengthened, and can look forward to pressure on the queenside and/or center, with a timely e6 being a continual threat, and f4-f5 looming in the background as a long-term danger for his opponent. At this point Black has: A 8...Qd5; B 8...Bb7.

A

	8	Qd5

This can lead to amazing complications, with some very pretty ideas for White.

9 g3

Already Black is faced with another fork: A1 9...Be6; A2 9...Bb7.

There are too many problems after 9...Bf5?! 10 Bg2 and now (a) 10... Be4? 11 0-0 e6 12 Re1 △ 13 Rxe4 (e.g. 13...c6 14 axb5, or even 14 Rxe4! Qxe4 15 Ne1 Qg6 16 axb5 with a wonderful attack); or (b) 10...e6 11 0-0 Qb7 12 Nh4 Be4, and now White has two excellent continuations: 13 Bxe4 Qxe4 14 Re1 Qb7 15 d5! Qxd5 16 Qxd5 exd5 17 axb5 Nd7 18 bxa6 Bc5 19 Be3 ± Gligoric - Buljovic, Novi Sad 1979; or 13 Qg4 "±" (Miles), when 13...Bxg2 14 Nxg2 g6 looks necessary, but White has great leeway, e.g. 15 Bg5 Nd7 16 Nf4! h6 17 Bf6 Nxf6 18 exf6 △ Re1.

A1

	9	Be6
	10 Bg2	Qb7
	11 0-0	

A transpositional possibility is 11 Ba3 Bd5 12 0-0 e6 13 Bxf8 Kxf8 14

Nh4 Bxg2 15 Nxg2 Nd7, which is analysed in the note to 12 e6 below.

White has an aggressive option in 11 Nh4!? Bd5 12 Bxd5 Qxd5 13 0-0 e6 14 Ng2! Nd7! 15 Nf4 Qb7 16 Qg4 ''±'' (Cafferty and Hooper) Sosonko - Schammo, Ostend 1975. This assessment is probably exaggerated, however, since 16...0-0-0! (only move) 17 axb5 axb5 18 Be3 Nb6 is complex (one idea for White might be 19 Ra5!? Nd5 20 Nxe6!? Nxe3 21 fxe3 fxe6 22 Qxe6† Kb8 23 Rfa1† etc.).

| 11 ..... | Bd5 |
| 12 e6!? | |

Now it's *White's* turn for a major choice. Also promising is 12 Ba3!? e6 (12...Nd7!? 13 Nh4(!) looks similar) 13 Bxf8 Kxf8 14 Nh4 Bxg2 15 Nxg2 Nd7!

Diagram 43

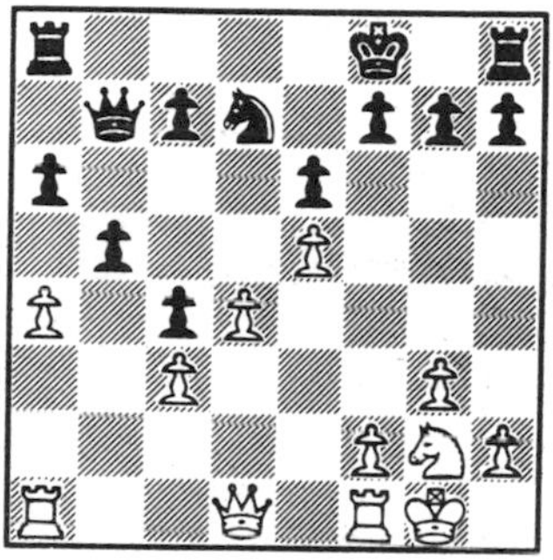

After 15...Nd7

And now:

(a) 16 Ne3 g6 17 f4 Nb6 with unclear prospects, Ivkov - Filip, Zagreb 1965;

(b) 16 f4!? f5? (16...g6 17 g4 f5 *Informant*; 17 Ne3 would be Ivkov - Filip again) 17 exf6 g6 (17...Nxf6 18 f5!) Chekhov - R. Bernard, Rostock 1984, and instead of 18 Qe2 Re8 19 axb5 axb5 20 Rfb1, which lead to a draw, *Informant* recommends 18 Qg4! Kf7 (18...Re8 19 f5!) 19 f5! exf5 20 Rxf5 ± △ Rxh5.

(c) 16 Qd2(!) was suggested by Karklins some years back, to prevent ...g6 before embarking upon f4-f5, and this seems an excellent idea, since ...h6 would be weakening, e.g. 16...h6 17 f4 g6 18 g4 etc..

| 12 ..... | Bxe6 |

Not 12...f6? 13 Nh4 ±. 12...fxe6 is plausible, but 13 Nh4 g6 14 Re1 (Balashov, threatening 15 Rxe6) looks pretty promising for White.

13 Ng5	Bd5
14 Bxd5	Qxd5
15 axb5	

Balashov - Miles, Bugojno 1978. Miles continued 15...axb5? 16 Rxa8 Qxa8 17 Qg4! and suddenly everything was falling apart:

(See diagram on page 31)

17...Nc6 (18 Qc8 mate is threatened, and 17...e6? 18 Nxe6 fxe6 19 Qxe6† Be7 20 Bg5 Nc6 21 Re1 is too strong; also unavailing are 17...Nd7 18 Nxf7! and 17...Qb7 18 Qf5 f6 19 Ne6 with a decisive bind.) 18 Qf3! (18 Qf5? Nd8) 18...f6 19 Ne6 Qb7 20 Qd5! g5 21 Bf4! Bh6 (21...gxf4 22 Qh5†) 22 Re1

Qb6 23 Nxc7† Kf8 24 Re6 gxf4 25 Rxc6 Qb8 26 Ne6† Ke8 27 Rc7 Kf7
28 Nxf4† Kf8 29 Qc5 1 - 0.

A fluent and effective attack. Black's best chance to improve comes on
move 15, when he has the options 15...h6 (e.g. 16 Nh3 e6 17 Nf4 Qd7 18
Qf3 with complications -- Balashov. Or 16 Qf3!? -- Gligoric -- when 16...Qxf3
17 Nxf3 △ Ne5, Nxc4 could follow: ±); or 15...e6!? 16 Re1 Bd6 (16...Be7
17 Re5! looks good, e.g. 17...Qb7 18 Qa4) 17 Qh5 g6 18 Qh6 "=/∞" (Balashov); this may well favor White after e.g. 18...Bf8 19 Qh3! Bg7 20 Bf4 with
designs on e6.

Thus 8...Qd5 9 g3 Be6 10 Bg2 Qb7 may not have a completely clear theoretical status, but between 11 Nh4 and the choice of 12 Ba3 or 12 e6 after 11
0-0 Bd5, Black cannot be happy with his defensive burdens. Thus the more
important move has become 9...Bb7:

A2

| | 9 ..... | Bb7 |
| | 10 Bg2 | Qd7 |

Diagram 45   After 10...Qd7

A popular position. White has: A21 11 Ba3; A22 11 Nh4.

11 0-0!? of Nemet - Hort, Lugano 1983 was original but slow: 11...e6
(11...Bd5? 12 e6! Qxe6 13 Ng5 Qd7 14 Bxd5 Qxd5 15 axb5 is one idea,
transposing to Balashov - Miles, above, or here 13 axb5 h6 14 Re1 is also possible, with attack) 12 Nh4 Bxg2 (12...c6 13 f4 =/∞ Hort) 13 Nxg2 b4!? 14
Nf4 Nc6 15 Qe2 bxc3 16 d5 ("∞" Hort) 16...exd5 17 e6 fxe6 18 Nxe6
Kf7 19 Re1 Kg8 and Black unravelled, although the game was drawn.

A21

11 Ba3

This is both the old move and, once again, the "new" move. White tries to
weaken Black on the dark squares.

                11 .....   Bd5

The natural 11...e6 12 Bxf8 Kxf8 13 0-0 of Bronstein - Korchnoi, Moscow
1964 has not been repeated, to my knowledge. That game went 13...g6 14
Nh4 "=/∞" (ECO); in fact White won nicely and rather convincingly: 14...c6
(14...Bxg2 15 Nxg2 c6 16 f4! Qc7 17 Qf3 Ra7 18 Ne3 △ 18...Nd7 19 g4!
h5 20 h3 △ f5 -- Karklins) 15 f4 Qe7 (15...Qc7 16 g4; 15...h5 16 Be4!
Karklins) 16 Qd2

(See the diagram on the next page)

40

Diagram 46

After 16 Qd2

16...Kg7 (16...Nd7 17 f5! exf5 18 Rxf5! gxf5 19 Qh6† is overwhelming -- Karklins) 17 f5! exf5 18 Rxf5 Bc8 19 Rf6 Ra7 20 Raf1 Be6 21 Qg5 Qe8 (21...Nd7? 22 Rxg6†; 21...Qd8 22 Be4) 22 Be4 Rg8 23 Ng2! Kh8 24 Nf4 Re7 25 axb5 axb5 26 Qh6! Nd7 27 Bxc6 b4 28 d5 Bg4 29 e6 Qf8 30 Qxf8 Nxf8 31 h3 g5 32 d6! and White won in a few moves. A beautiful game.

Black has an obvious try for improvement by 13...Nc6!?, to play 14...Ne7. But then White seems to have two good replies. Sometime back I analysed 14 Ng5 (△Ne4-c5) 14...Rb8 (14...Nd8 15 axb5 ± may be better, but not much) 15 Ne4 Ba8 16 Nc5 Qc8 17 axb5 axb5 18 f4 Ne7 19 Qd2 Bxg2 20 Qxg2 and Black is very unhappy, e.g. 20...Nd5? 21 f5! Ne3? 22 Qc6!. Recently I found an analysis by Karklins which runs 13...Nc6 14 Nh4 Nd8 (perhaps not best; 14...Rb8!?) 15 Bxb7 Nxb7 16 axb5 Qxb5 17 Qf3 Qd5 18 Qxd5 exd5 19 Rfb1 Nd8 20 Ra5 c6 21 Rb6 or 21 Nf5.

Finally, a game Inkiov - Bellon, Rome 1985 saw 13...Bd5!? 14 Nh4 c6 15 Qh5 h6 16 Bxd5! cxd5 (else 17 f4) 17 axb5 g6 18 Qf3 Kg7 19 Qf6† Kh7 20 f4! ± with a very strong attack.

The lines following 11...e6 strike me as tremendously instructive.

                12 0-0   Nc6
13 e6 was a threat.

                13 Re1   g6
13...b4? 14 e6! ("±±" Hort) isn't good: 14...Bxe6 15 Ne5 Nxe5 16 Bxa8 Nd3 17 cxb4 Nxe1 18 d5! Bxd5 19 Bxd5, or 14...fxe6 15 cxb4, White is much better.

But 13...Rb8!? is still highly controversial:

Diagram 47

After 13...Rb8

In reply, White has a choice which proves to be a subtle one:

(a) van der Sterren - Hort, Amsterdam 1982 went 14 axb5!? axb5. Then Hort likes "15 Qe2! ±", although after 15...e6 16 Bxf8 Kxf8, I don't see it. A little better looks 15 Ng5!?, in order to reply to 15...e6 with 16 Bxd5 Qxd5 and 17 Qh5 or perhaps 17 Bxf8 Kxf8 18 Qh5 (e.g. 18...Qd7 19 Re4 △ 19... Nd8 20 Nxh7† or 19...h6 20 Nxf7!).

Van der Sterren continued most logically with 15 e6!? fxe6 ("only move" – Hort; 15...Bxe6 16 d5!? Bxd5 17 Ne5 Nxe5 18 Bxd5 Nd3(!) 19 Qf3 Nxe1 20 Rxe1 Rb6 seems to hold, and here 16 Ne5!? Nxe5 17 Rxe5 Bg4 is unclear; so probably 16 Ng5 Bd5 17 Ne4!, or here 16...Bf5 17 Qf3 Nd8 18 d5! should be tried)

Diagram 48

After 15...fxe6

16 Ne5(?) 16...Nxe5 17 Rxe5 Bxg2 18 Kxg2 g6 19 Qe2 Bg7 20 Rxe6 0-0 21 Rxe7 Qc6† = △ 22 Kg1 Rfe8 or 22 Qe4 Qxe4† 23 Rxe4 Rf7 = .

This certainly doesn't look bad for Black (excepting perhaps 15 Ng5!?), and yet the White attack is again deceptively strong. There are at least three improvements on move 16:

(a1) 16 Ng5 Bxg2 17 Kxg2 Qd5† 18 Qf3! of Veingold - Kasparov, USSR 1984, and now Veingold shows a way for Black to escape with 18...Nd8 19 Nxe6 Qxf3† 20 Kxf3 Nxe6 21 Rxe6 Ra8! 22 d5 ("±"), but White is still better; compare '(b)' below.

(a2) 16 Bh3(!) looks very promising to me, e.g. 16...g6 17 Ng5 Nd8 18 Qc2! etc..

(a3) "16 Qe2!" (Veingold) is similar and also good, e.g. 16...h5 17 Bh3 Rh6 18 Ng5 ± (Veingold).

(b) As if that weren't convincing, White has a possible finesse by 14 e6!?, whose points show up nicely in the line 14...fxe6 15 Ng5 Bxg2 16 Kxg2 Qd5† 17 Qf3 b4 18 Bxb4!! Nxb4 19 cxb4 Qxg5 20 Qc6† "with attack" (Veingold). Play could go 20...Kf7 (20...Kd8? 21 Re5! and 22 d5) 21 Qxe6† Ke8 22 Qc6† Kf7 23 Qxc4† Ke8 24 Qxc7 Rd8 25 Re5 and 26 Rae1 with a winning game.

For these reasons, 13...Rb8 looks inadequate, and yet the text (13...g6) may not be a major improvement:

(See the diagram on the next page)

14 Bc5

Diagram 49   After 13...g6

Here, for example, 14 e6!? fxe6 15 Ng5! (Hort gives 15 Ne5 Nxe5 16 Bxd5 exd5 17 Rxe5 e6 in a note) 15...Bxg2 (15...b4!?; 15...Nd8!?) 16 Kxg2! deserves notice, e.g. 16...Qd5† 17 Qf3 Qxf3† 18 Kxf3, and now Loginov - Nadyrhanov, USSR 1983 continued 18...Nd8 19 Nxe6 Nxe6 20 Rxe6 Kd7 21 d5 Rg8 22 Bc5 bxa4 23 Rxa4 c6 24 Rxc6 e6 25 Bd4 exd5 26 Rcxa6 Rxa6 27 Rxa6 Be7 28 h4 ±. This looks good, but the text, which is more solid, has been preferred in practice.

14 .....   **Rd8**

14...Rb8 (not again!) 15 axb5 axb5 16 Ng5 Bxg2 17 Kxg2 Bh6 18 e6! Qd5† 19 Qf3 Qxf3† 20 Nxf3 f6 21 d5 ("±" Ehlvest) 21...Ne5 22 Nxe5 fxe5 23 Rxe5 Bg7 24 Re3 Bf6 25 Ra7 Kd8 (25...Rd8 26 Rxc7 Rxd5 27 Bb4 Ehlvest) 26 Kf3 (△ Ke4, Bd4) 26...g5 27 Ke4 g4 28 f4 gxf3 29 Rxf3 Rg8 30 Bb4 Kc8 31 Rf5 Rb7 32 Ra8† Rb8 33 Ra1 Rb7 34 Ra6! Kb8 35 Rh5 Rg7 36 Kf5 c5 37 dxc6 Rc7 38 Kf4 1 - 0 Ehlvest - Chekov, USSR Ch 1984. Compare what follows.

15 axb5   **axb5**

16 Ng5   **Bxg2**

17 e6!

With the rook on d8, the trick with 17 Kxg2 Bh6!? 18 e6?! (18 Nxf7? Qd5†) 18...Qd5† 19 Qf3? Bxg5 doesn't work (compare the last note), and here 19 Nf3 fxe6 20 Rb1 0-0! 21 Rxb5 Rf7 is also strong. Thus White's combination.

Diagram 50   After 17 e6

17 .....   **fxe6**

And *here,* had Black his rook on b8, Black could try 17...Qd5 18 exf7† Kd8 etc.; but as it stands, 17...Qd5?? 18 exf7† Kd7 19 Qg4† e6 20 Nxe6 is

43

devastating.

18	Kxg2	Qd5†
19	Qf3!	

The same idea we've seen before. White forces an endgame where Black's split pawns and lack of development will doom him if he can't make a quick, liquidating pawn break.

19	.....	Qxf3†

19...e5!? is well answered by 20 Qxd5 Rxd5 21 Ra8†, e.g. 21...Kd7 22 Nf7 Rg8 23 dxe5! etc., and 20 dxe5! Qxf3† 21 Kxf3 also seems to win.

20	Kxf3	Rd5

Now on 20...e5, 21 Ne6 Rd7 22 d5 Nd8 23 Rxe5 is easiest.

21	Nxe6	Kd7
22	Re2?!	

Olafsson's 22 Re4! Bh6 23 Ra2 threatening moves like g4, h4, and Rae2 is more accurate. After the text, H. Olafsson - Hort, Thessaloniki 1984 went 22...Bh6 23 Rae1 Ra8 24 g4 Bg5? (24...b4! 25 cxb4 c3 26 g5! [26 b5 Ne5†] 26...Bxg5 = Olafsson. With the rooks on e4 and e2, White could simply respond to ...b4 with Bxb4) 25 Nxg5 Rxg5 26 Bxe7 Rd5 27 Bc5 b4 28 Ke4! Rg5 29 cxb4 Rxg4† 30 Kd5! ("±") 30...Rb8 31 Kxc4 Rxd4† 32 Bxd4 Rxb4† 33 Kc5 Rxd4 34 Re7† Nxe7 35 Kxd4 and White went on to win the ending.

A22

11 Nh4

"!" (Miles), although it hasn't been used since. We will follow Kavalek - Miles, Wijk aan Zee 1978:

11	.....	c6

11...Bxg2 12 Nxg2 e6 13 Qf3 Ra7 14 axb5 Qxb5 15 Nf4 ± △ d5 (Miles); compare the notes in the line 11 Ba3 e6 above. More natural here is 12...c6, but either 13 Ba3 or 13 0-0 e6 14 Ne3 △ f4-f5 is strong.

12	f4	e6
13	f5!	exf5
14	0-0	g6
15	Bg5	

"±" (Miles). Now he gives 15...Bg7 16 Bf6 0-0? 17 Nxf5 gxf5 18 Qh5 h6 19 Rxf5 ± △ Rg5; and instead of 16...0-0, he recommends 16...Kf8. But in that case White has more than enough play, e.g. 17 Qd2! h6 18 Rae1 Qe6 19 g4! Bxf6 20 gxf5 gxf5 21 exf6 Qxf6 22 Nxf5 with a terrific attack (Re7, Qf4-c7, and Qb2-a3 being typical threats). Thus:

15	.....	Be7
16	Bf6	Rg8
17	Qd2	Qe6
18	axb5	Bxf6

18...axb5 19 Rxa8 Bxa8 20 Ra1 Bb7 21 Ra7 Qc8 22 Bxe7 Kxe7 23 d5 Rd8 24 Qg5† Ke8 25 d6 Rd7 26 Nxf5 ± (Miles) is a lengthy but forced line.

19	gxf6	Qxf6
20	Rae1†	Kd8

And now Miles' suggestion 21 Qh6! ± △ Nxf5 is very strong, e.g. 21...Qg7

22 Qf4 (22...Qf6 23 b6!). The game went 21 bxc6?! Bxc6 22 d5 Bd7! 23 Nf3 Re8 24 Rb1 Bb5 25 Nd4 Nd7 26 g4 Qd6 27 gxf5 f6 28 Qh6 Ne5, and still White had 29 Qxh7! ±, but time trouble intervened and he actually lost.

The burden of proof is on Black after both 11 Ba3 and 11 Nh4. I have gone into great detail to illustrate 8...Qd5, since it is the most direct and logical way to contest the light squares.

B

8	Bb7

This would obviously be the ideal move (it is again "in the news" of late), but Black allows the serious thrust:

9 e6!

Diagram 51

After 9 e6

Now Black has to decide between a broken-up kingside and a cramped position: B1 9...fxe6; B2 9...f6.

B1

9	fxe6
10 Be2!	

10 Ng5!? Qd5 (10...Qd6 11 Qg4 Nd7 12 Bf4 Nf6 13 Bxd6 Nxg4 17 Bxc7 ± Lehman - van Scheltinga, Beverwijk 1966) 11 Qg4 Qt5 12 Qg3 e5! 13 Qxe5 Qxe5 14 dxe5 of Bronstein - Chikovani, USSR 1967 is also not bad, but perhaps not so convincing after 14...e6 15 Nxe6 Kd7 (Neistadt; ± ?).

10	Qd5
11 Ng5!	

Theory considers 11 Bf4 Nd7 12 Bxc7 g6 and 11 Be3 Nd7 12 Ng5 unclear.

11	Qxg2
12 Rf1	Bd5

12...Qxh2?! 13 Nxe6 threatens Bf4, e.g. 13...Qd6 14 d5! △ 15 Bf4.

13 axb5	

(See diagram on the next page)

13	axb5

The alternatives are 13...g6 14 bxa6 Bh6 15 Nxe6! Bxc1 16 Nxc7† Kd8 17 Nxd5 Qxd5 18 Qxc1 ± Vranesic - Clarke, Havana 1966; or 13...Qxh2 14 Bg4! h5 (14...Qd6 15 Ba3) 15 Bxe6 Bxe6 16 Qf3! c6 17 Nxe6 Qd6 18 Qf5 with a crushing attack, Doroskevich - Antoshin, USSR 1967.

14 Rxa8	Bxa8
15 Bg4!	

Diagram 52

After 13 axb5

Also advantageous, but perhaps less so, was 15 Bf4!? g6 16 Nxe6 Na6 17 Qa1 Bb7 18 Qa5 in Bronstein - Lavdansky, USSR 1965.

After 15 Bg4!, Knaak - Bönsch, East Germany 1970 went simply 15...e5 (15...Qxh2 16 Bxe6! ± ECO) 16 Be6! ±, a sample line going 16...Bd5 17 Bh3! Qxh2 18 Qh5† Kd8 19 Qg4 etc.. Black's light squares fall without compensation in these lines.

B2

9 .....   f6

Recently revived, but this is also very risky.

Diagram 53

After 9...f6

10 Be2

This move was a smashing success in its debut, but White seems to have one good alternative:

(a) **10 g3?!** appears too slow, the main line going 10...Qd5 11 Bg2 Qxe6† 12 Be3 c6! (Not 12...Nd7? 13 axb5 axb5 14 Ng5! Najdorf - Mendes, 1958. 12...Qc8!? 13 d5!? is interesting, e.g. 13...e6 14 Nh4 g6 15 dxe6 Bxg2 16 Nxg2 Qxe6 17 Nf4 etc.. Vaiser - Korsunsky, USSR 1978 went 12...Qc8 13 0-0 e6 14 Nh4 Bxg2 15 Nxg2 Bd6, and now 16 axb5 Nd7 17 bxa6 Rxa6 18 Qh5† g6 19 Qb5 ± wins back White's material. In this line, 14 Re1!? is also possible) 13 0-0 Qc8 14 Re1 Kf7! 15 axb5 axb5 16 Rxa8 Bxa8 17 Qe2 Na6 18 Bf4 Bronstein - Byrne, Helsinki 1952 ("=/∞" ECO). It's not easy to untangle, and the game was eventually drawn. Nevertheless, this is not a very compelling line in view of the alternatives.

(b) **10 Be3(!)** is much better, and perhaps as good as the text: 10...Qd5 11

46

Qb1! (11 axb5!? axb5 12 Rxa8 Bxa8 13 Qb1 is also interesting, or here even 13 Qa1!?) 11...g6 (11...c6 12 Nd2! △Bxc4 is awkward for Black, and 11... Qxe6 12 axb5 Bxf3 13 gxf3 Nd7 14 Qb4 regains the pawn with threats) 12 Be2 Bg7 13 axb5 axb5 14 Rxa8 Bxa8 15 Nd2 (!! again △Bxc4) 15...Bc6 (?, but e.g. 15...Qxg2?? 16 Qxb5† and 15...c6 16 Qa2! are also bad) 16 Bf3! △16...Qxe6 17 d5! or 16...Qd6 17 Nxc4 or 16...Qf5 17 Qxf5! gxf5 18 d5 Bb7 19 d6! etc. (19...Bxf3 20 dxc7 ±).

To all appearances, 10 Be3 is a very tough move to meet.

| 10 ..... | Qd5 |

(a) 10...g6 11 0-0 Bg7 12 Ba3 0-0 13 Nd2 △Bf3 gives White "a very promising game" (Christiansen);

(b) 10...Bd5 11 Bf4 (11 0-0!?) 11...g6 12 axb5 axb5 (12...Bxe6 13 Qa4) 13 Rxa8 Bxa8 14 Qa1 Bd5 (14...Nc6 15 d5) 15 Qa5 "and White has ample compensation" (Sosonko).

| 11 0-0 | Qxe6 |
| 12 Re1 | Qd7 |

12...g6 13 Nd2 (Sosonko).

| 13 Nh4 |

13 Nd2 Bd5! 14 Bf3 e6 15 axb5 Be7 = (Sosonko).

13	g6
14 Bg4	f5
15 Bf3	Nc6
16 Bg5!

Diagram 54   After 16 Bg5

| 16 ..... | h6 |

Suddenly Black is helpless before the White onslaught, e.g.:

(a) 16...0-0-0 17 axb5 axb5 18 Qb1 Nb8 19 Bxb7 Kxb7 20 Qa2 and wins (Sosonko);

(b) 16...Kf7 17 d5 Nd8 18 Ra2 h6 19 Bf4 Bg7 20 Bh5! gxh5 21 Qxh5† Kg8 22 Nxf5 and wins (Sosonko).

| 17 d5!? |

17 Nxg6! hxg5 18 d5! Nd8 19 Ne5 is stronger and wins (Belyavsky).

| 17 ..... | Ne5 |

17...hxg5 18 Nxg6 Rh7 (18...Nd8 is the last note) 19 dxc6 Qxd1 20 Rxd1 Bc8 21 Nxf8 Kxf8 22 Rd8† Kg7 23 axb5 "was not too hopeful" (Christiansen).

18	Rxe5	hxg5
19	Nxg6	Qd6

19...Rh6 20 Nxf8 Kxf8 21 Qd2 (Sosonko) or 19...g4 20 Bxg4! fxg4 21 Nxh8 Bg7 22 Rh5 0-0-0 23 Nf7 Rf8 24 Ne5 ± (Christiansen). Best 19... Rg8! 20 Nxf8 Rxf8 21 Bh5† Kd8 22 Qd2 (Sosonko).

20	Nxh8	Qxe5
21	d6!	Rd8

21...Bxf3 22 d7†; 21...Qxh8 22 Bxb7 Rd8 23 dxc7!; 21...0-0-0 22 d7† Rxd7 23 Bxb7† Kxb7 24 Qxd7 Qxc3 25 Rd1 Qxh8 26 axb5, all ± (Christiansen).

22	Bh5†!	1 - 0

Due to 22...Kd7 23 dxe7† Kxe7 24 Ng6† Ke6 25 Qxd8 etc..

Thus 7...Nxc3 and 8...Bb7 is on the retreat. In general, Black's traditional main line with 4...a6 doesn't seem to be holding up, and I can unhesitatingly recommend White's position after 5 e4.

VI 4...c6: Introduction and 7...Bf5

1	d4	d5
2	c4	dxc4
3	Nf3	Nf6
4	Nc3	c6

Now we have a Slav Defense. It is also possible to use 4 Nc3 versus the regular Slav order, i.e. 1 d4 d5 2 c4 c6 3 Nf3 Nf6 4 Nc3 and if now 4...e6 (instead of 4...dxc4), 5 e3 or 5 Bg5 is a main line Semi-Slav. One should note the line 4...Bf5(?!) 5 cxd5! Nxd5 (5...cxd5 6 Qb3 Bc8 7 Bf4 a6 8 Rc1 Nc6 9 Ne5 [or 9 e3 ±] 9...Nxd4 10 Qa4† Nc6 11 e4! ± Uhlmann - Muflung, Moscow 1956) 6 e3 (or 6 Nd2!?, as in Kostic - Euwe, Budapest 1921) 6...e6 7 Bd3 Bxd3 8 Qxd3 Nbd7 9 0-0 Be7 10 e4 N5f6 11 Bg5 h6 12 Be3 0-0 13 Rad1 Qc7 14 h3 ±/± Spassov - Knudson, Silkeborg 1983.

5 e4

This is sometimes called the Geller Gambit. Of course 5 a4 is the traditional main line, but here, as after 4...a6, 5 e4 launches a very dangerous and at the least unrefuted attack. This has again achieved a certain prominence due to Kasparov's use in some nice victories. I should point out that, *in principle,* 4...c6 5 e4 seems to me less effective for White than 4...a6 5 e4, if only because Black has the opportunity of mobilizing his queenside pawns more quickly than in the latter case. Nevertheless, we shall see that 4...c6 leaves White with other advantages, and I think top players might be surprised to see how good White's chances really are. Of course many Queen's Gambit Accepted advocates aren't interested in playing the Slav Defense at all, so if 5 e4 doesn't appeal, one may be effective with 5 a4 also.

5 .....   b5

Anything else cedes the c-pawn without compensation for White's center.

6	e5	Nd5
7	a4	

Diagram 55

After 7 a4

This is of course similar to what we've seen in the last 3 chapters, but now aside from 7...a6 8 axb5 Nxc3 (transposing to Chapter IV), Black has some options.

7 .....   Bf5!?

A very interesting idea. Other moves are 7...e6 (see Chapters 7 and 8), and these:

(a) 7...b4? 8 Ne4 (±) 8...c3!? 9 bxc3 bxc3 10 Qb3 ±;

49

(b) 7...Bb7?! 8 e6! f6 9 g3 Qd6 10 Bh3 ± Najdorf - Ojanen, Helsinki 1952;

(c) 7...Be6 (?! ECO) 8 Ng5! (8 axb5!? Nxc3 9 bxc3 cxb5 10 Ng5 Bd5 11 e6 fxe6 12 Qg4 h5 13 Qf4 Qd6 14 Qf7† Kd8 Tolush - Smyslov, USSR Ch 1947 is held to be good for Black, but 15 Bf4 e5 16 dxe5 Bxf7 17 Nxf7† Ke8 18 Nxd6† or 17 exd6 Bg8 18 Rd1 exd6 19 g3 seems to favor White slightly) 8... Nxc3 9 bxc3 Bd5 (9...Qd7 10 axb5 cxb5 11 Nxe6 Qxe6 12 Qf3 Nc6 13 Ra6 Rc8 14 Be2 ±) 10 e6 is assessed as "±" by Taimanov. Then a possible line would be 10...fxe6 11 Qg4 h5 12 Qf4 Qd6! 13 Qf7† Kd8 14 Bf4 e5 (14...Qd7 15 Be5!) 15 dxe5 Bxf7 16 Nxf7† Ke8 17 Nxd6† exd6 18 exd6 with advantage, e.g. 18...g5!? 19 Bxg5 Bxd6 20 0-0-0 ± intending g3.

(d) After 7...Nxc3 8 bxc3, ECO gives 8...Be6 9 Be2 leading to equality, but fails to note that 9 Ng5! transposes to the analysis in '(c)', which favors White And 8...e6 9 g3 (or 9 axb5 axb5 10 Ng5 Bb7 11 Qh5, which is the main line with 7...e6) 9...Bb7 10 Bg2 a6 11 Ng5! Be7 12 Ne4 led to a big advantage in Gelks - Zagarovsky, USSR 1948. White has moves like Qg4 (...g6), Bh6, and 0-0 with f4-f5 or in some cases Ba3 to work with.

The only truly independent idea with 7...Nxc3 8 bxc3 is 8...h6!? 9 g3 (9 Be2!? Be6 10 0-0 Bd5 Krogius - Saposhnikov, USSR 1959, and 11 Ne1 △ Nc2-e3 and e.g. f4-f5 is recommended as "=/∞" by ECO. In that case, White has definite attacking chances) 9...Be6 10 Bg2 Bd5, and now simply 11 Ba3(!) e6 12 Bxf8 Kxf8 13 0-0 intending Nh4 with f4-f5 looks promising, with play very much as in the 4...a6 lines.

8 axb5!   Nb4!

The only sequence played here to date has been 8...Nxc3(?) 9 bxc3 cxb5 10 Ng5! e6 (forced, in view of 11 Qf3, e.g. 10...Nd7 11 Qf3 e6 12 Nxf7! Kxf7 13 g4 etc.) 11 g4! Bg6 (11...Qd5 has two refutations: 12 Rg1 Be4 13 Be3! ± △ Ne4, and 12 gxf5! Qxh1 13 fxe6 fxe6 14 Qg4 ± etc.) 12 Bg2 Nd7 13 f4! (△ 14 Qf3 and 15 f5) 13...Be7 (13...h6 14 f5! exf5 15 gxf5 Bxf5 16 Qf3 ± Inkiov) 14 Qf3 0-0 (14...Bxg5 15 Qxa8 ±±) 15 h4 Bd3 16 f5 exf5 (16...h6 17 Qxa8! ± Inkiov) 17 gxf5 Nb6 18 Qg4 Qc8 19 Be4! Bxe4 20 Qxe4 ± Inkiov - Padevsky, Pamporovo 1982, and instead of 20...g6? 21 0-0 f6 22 Ne6 fxe5 23 Nxf8 Bxf8 24 Ra2 (or 24 dxe5 ±±) 24...exd4 25 fxg6 Qe8 26 gxh7† Kh8 27 Qg4 Bc5 28 Rg2! 1 - 0, Black had to play 20...f6 21 Ne6 Rf7 22 Rg1 ± (Inkiov).

8...Nb4! forces the following critical line given by Lilienthal without analysis:

9 Bxc4   Nc2†
10 Ke2   Nxa1
11 Qa4

(See diagram on the next page)

White has only a pawn for his rook, but threatens to regain the knight on a1 or, more powerfully, to play bxc6 and e.g. d5, Nd5, or Nb5 as required. An objective assessment is hard to come by because of the variety of possible defenses, but here are the two best lines I've found for Black:

(a) 11...Bd7 is the more forcing idea: 12 e6 fxe6 13 Ne5 cxb5 14 Bxb5 (This is equivalent to 11...cxb5 12 Bxb5† Bd7 13 e6 fxe6 14 Ne5) 14...a6! (14...Bxb5 15 Nxb5 Nd7 16 Bf4! threatens both Nc6 and Rxa1), and now 15 d5!? gives good chances in lines like 15...Bxb5† 16 Nxb5 Nd7 17 dxe6!

Diagram 56

After 11 Qa4

or 15...exd5 16 Qf4 Qc7 17 Bxd7† Nxd7 18 Qf7† Kd8 19 Bf4! (e.g. 19...
Rb8! 20 Qxd5!? Rxb2† 21 Kd3! ±), but 15...axb5! 16 Qxa8 b4! (16...Nc2
17 Rd1!; 16...Nb3 17 Be3!) 17 dxe6!? Bxe6 leaves White with only speculative tires. So he should probably continue 15 Bxd7† Nxd7 16 Rd1! Nb3!
(versus d5; 16...Nc2 17 d5 Qc7 18 Bf4!) 17 Be3!? (17 Qxb3!? Nxe5 18
dxe5 Qc8 19 Qa5† Kf7 20 Rd3!?), and the threat of 18 d5 compels an immediate response, e.g. 18...Na5 19 d5 Nc4 20 Nxc4! or 18...Rc8 19 d5
Nbc5 20 Bxc5 Rxc5 21 b4! (or 21 f4!?), or 18...Qc7 19 f4!? Rd8 20 d5
exd5 21 Nxd5 Qc2† 22 Ke1 e6 23 Nb6 with a great attack. This just
scratches the surface, however, and who knows if such a speculative attack is
objectively sound? For the practical player willing to take a risk (or willing
to prepare very thoroughly), this line is reasonable. The same may be said for:

(b) 11...Nd7!? 12 e6!? fxe6 (12...Nb6?? 13 exf7† ⧺; 12...Bxe6 13 Bxe6
fxe6 14 bxc6 Nb6 15 Qxa1 unclear, e.g. 15...Qd6 16 Qa5! Qxc6 17 Ne5
Qd6 18 Bf4) 13 Qxa1 Nb6 14 Bb3 cxb5 15 Nxb5 and White's compensation
is definitely there (Bf4, Ne5 are ideas and the Black king is exposed), but it's
not clear how much is needed to offset the loss of an exchange.

The other order is 11...Nd7 12 Qxa1(!), e.g. 12...Nb6 13 Bb3 cxb5 14
Nxb5. White gains fewer squares thereby, but he gets an extra pawn, and 14...
e6? can be answered by 15 Ba4!. On 14...a6 15 Nc3 e6, 16 Rd1! and d5
next continues the attack.

In conclusion, the line with 7...Bf5 offers White good attacking chances,
but it will take more research to see what the proper result of this attack
should be. See also the comments at the end of Chapter VIII.

VII 7...e6 Gambit With 11...Qd7

1 d4	d5
2 c4	dxc4
3 Nf3	Nf6
4 Nc3	c6
5 e4	b5
6 e5	Nd5
7 a4	e6

This is the main line for Black, by which he secures his center and prevents e6 once and for all.

8 axb5	Nxc3

An alternative which first appeared just a few years back is 8...Bb4!?

Diagram 57   8...Bb4

In the game Nikolic - Matulovic, 9 Bd2!? got a bad name after 9...Bxc3 10 bxc3 cxb5 11 Ng5 Bb7 12 h4? (12 Qh5 Qe7 13 Ne4 0-0 14 Bg5 f6 15 exf6 gxf6 16 Bh6 Rf7 17 Be2 Nd7 18 0-0 "=/∞" Matulovic; here 15...Nxf6 should also be considered; note also 13 Nxh7 Qf8!. But the main problem with this line seems to be 13 Ne4 Nf4! etc., so White should consider simply 13 f3 △Ne4) 12...Nd7 13 Qh5 Qe7 14 Ne4 0-0 15 Nd6 Bc6 16 Rh3 f6! ∓ Nikolic - Matulovic, Yugoslavia 1982. Once he is committed to 9 Bd2, 11 Qb1!? a6 12 Qe4 or 12 Ng5 Bb7 13 Be2 h6 14 Ne4 0-0 15 Bf3 etc. is an alternative way of playing worth considering.

White found a more promising answer in Petursson - Valkesalmi, Hamar 1983/4: 9 Qa4(!) a5 (9...Bxc3† 10 bxc3 Nxc3 11 Qxc4 Nxb5 12 Qa4! ±) 10 Bd2 0-0 (10...Nb6!? 11 Qc2 Bxc3 12 bxc3! cxb5 13 Ng5 "with compensation for the pawn" -- Petursson. This is worth examing, e.g. 13...h6(?) 14 Ne4 0-0 15 Bxh6! f5 16 Bg5 etc.) 11 bxc6 Nb6 12 Qc2 f5! (12...Nxc6 13 Qe4! Petrusson) 13 exf6 gxf6 14 Be2 (14 g3!?) 14...Nxc6 Bb7 16 Rad1 Kh8 17 Ne4 Bxd2 (17...Be7 18 Nc5) 18 Qxd2 Ne7 19 Nc5 Bd5 20 Nh4! Rg8 21 g3 Ng6 22 Nxg6† Rxg6 23 Qe3 Qd6 24 Bh5! Rg7 25 Bf3 Rb8 26 Rfe1 Nd7 27 Bxd5 exd5 28 Qf3! Nxc5 29 dxc5 Qxc5 30 Rxd5 Qb6 31 Rd2 a4 32 Red1 with a large advantage due to the d-file and Black's exposed pawns.

9 bxc3	cxb5
10 Ng5	Bb7
11 Qh5	

(See diagram on the next page)

Diagram 58   After 11 Qh5

The basic gambit position. With threats of mate and Nxe6, Black has only 11...Qd7, which is the subject of this chapter, and 11...g6. The latter plan has a better reputation, but this may be based on some faulty assumptions, both about the strength of 11...g6 (White's attack is very strong -- see Chapter VIII) and about the weakness of 11...Qd7 (White's well-known wins have obscured the issue).

11	Qd7

Black avoids the weakening of the dark squares which 11...g6 entails. On the dark side, he restricts his queen to defense and allows White an extra tempo for attack.

12 Be2!

With the idea of 13 Nxh7. The immediate 12 Nxh7!? has two good replies: 12...Qd5!? 13 Nf6† gxf6 14 Qxh8 b4! Bagirov - Demirhanijian, USSR 1963, and 12...Nc6! e.g. 13 Nxf8? Rxh5? (13...Qxd4!! ∓ Kasparov; 14 Qxh8 Qxc3† or 14 cxd4 Rxh5 15 Nxe6 fxe6 16 Be3 0-0-0) 14 Nxd7 Kxd7 15 Rb1 a6 (? 15...Ba6!?) 16 Bxc4 Na5 17 Bf1 and White went on to win in Kasparov - Kupreichik, USSR Ch 1979.

Diagram 59   After 12 Be2

12	h6!?

Probably not best, but a nice example follows from it. Others from the diagram:

(a) 12...Bxg2? 13 Rg1 Bd5 14 Nxh7 Kd8 15 Nxf8! Rxf8 16 Rxg7 ±;

(b) 12...Na6 13 d5! (13 Nxh7 0-0-0 14 Nxf8 Rfxd8 15 Qg4, slightly ±, Zaitsev - Mnacakanian, USSR 1963) 13...g6 (13...exd5? 14 e6; 13...Nc7 14 d6 Nd5 15 Nxh7 ± Prandstetter. Perhaps 13...Nc5!?, but 14 d6 should keep an

53

advantage) 14 dxe6 fxe6 15 Qh3!? (15 Qg4! Nc7 16 0-0 h5 17 Qg3 ± Prand-stetter) 15...Nc7 16 0-0 Be7 17 Rd1 Bd5 Trapl - Makry, Czechoslovakian Ch 1982, and White still had 18 Bh5! with the ideas 18...Bxg5 19 Bxg6† or 18... 0-0-0 19 Bf3! Bc5 20 Ne4 ± or 18...Rf8 19 Nxh7 gxh5 20 Qxh5† Kd8 (20... Rf7 21 Qg6! △ Bh6) 21 Nxf8 Bxf8 22 Be3 a5 23 Rd4! ± △ Rf4-f7, Qg6, h4-h5-h6, etc. (Prandstetter).

(c) 12...Bd5(!) is a move Kasparov mentions, which succeeded nicely in the game McCambridge - Choobak, Pasadena 1983: 13 Nxh7 (13 Bf3!? [△ Bxd5, e6] 13...g6 14 Qh3 Nc6 15 0-0 and Ne4 and/or Bxd5 △ Re1 should be con-sidered) 13...Nc6 14 Nxf8 (14 Nf6† gxf6 15 Qxh8 fxe5!, and 16 Ba3!? b4! 17 Bxb4 Nxb4 18 cxb4 exd4! 19 Qxd4 Bxg2! 20 Qxd7† Kxd7 21 Rg1 Bb4† 22 Kd1 Bd5, or 16 Bh6 Qe7 17 Bxf8 [17 h4!? Kd7 18 Bg5!?] 17... Qxf8 18 Qxf8† Kxf8 with good play for Black) 14...Rxf8 15 Qg5 a5! (15... b4!? 16 0-0 b3? 17 Ba3! led to a draw in I. Rogers - Kirov, Biel 1984, but Rogers calls this "±" △ f4-f5) 16 0-0!? (16 Qxg7 0-0-0 17 Bg5 Rg8 18 Qf6!?; for 16 h4!?, see the note at the end) 16...Qe7 17 Qxg7 Kd7! 18 Qg5 (18 Bg5 Rg8!) 18...Qxg5 19 Bxg5 Rg8 20 h4 b4 and Black's pawns eventually decided

A very hard game to assess, with so many options for both sides. Aside from the possible improvement on White's 13th, a key juncture comes at the 16th move, when e.g. 16 h4!? is very interesting, e.g. 16...Qe7 17 Qxg7 in-tending Bg5, or 16...f6 17 exf6 gxf6 18 Qg6† Kd8 (18...Qf7 19 Bh5) 19 Bh6 etc. (19...Qf7 20 h5 Qxg6 21 hxg6 Rg8 22 Bh5 Bxg2 23 Rh4!?).

White has not yet established anything definite versus 12...Bd5, and it is an example of how the gambit is less clearly effective against 4...c6 than against 4...a6. Both sides should pay close attention to these "irregular" lines.

13 Bf3   Nc6

Not 13...hxg5? 14 Qxh8 Bxf3 15 Ba3!, and 13...g6?! also has its draw-backs: 14 Qh3 Nc6 15 Ne4 Be7 16 0-0 a5 17 Bf4 Rad8 18 Nd6† ± Szabo - Orendy, Hungarian Ch 1961.

Diagram 60

After 13...Nc6

14 0-0(!)

This is clearer than 14 d5!? Nxe5!? 15 dxe6 Nxf3† 16 Qxf3 fxe6 17 Qh5† Ke7 ∞, or here 14...hxg5!? 15 dxc6 Bxc6 16 Qxh8 Bxf3 17 gxf3 Qd3! unclear (Kasparov). 14 Ne4 Nxd4!? 15 cxd4 Bb4† 16 Bd2 Bxd2† 17 Nxd2 Qxd4 18 0-0 Bxf3 19 Nxf3 Qb6 ½ - ½ was Yermolinsky - Chernin, USSR 1982. Black's pawns are terribly strong, but his king may be hard to defend. Of course these lines leave room for improvements along the way.

54

14	.....	Nd8
15	Ne4	a5
16	Bg5	Bd5
17	Rfe1!	Nc6

Black's problems are mounting; Kasparov gives 17...Qb7 18 Bxd8! Kxd8 19 Nc5! Bxc5 20 Bxd5 Qxd5 21 dxc5 ±.

| 18 | Bh4 | Ra7 |
| 19 | Qg4 | Rh7?! |

Kasparov suggests 19...Bxe4 20 Bxe4 g5!?, but assesses this as ±, here 20... Ne7 21 d5! exd5 22 e6 is worse still. After 19...Rh7, Kasparov - Petursson, Malta 1980 continued 20 Nd6† Bxd6 21 Bxd5 Be7 22 Be4 g6 23 Bf6! Kf8 (23...Bxf6 24 gxf6 Kf8 might be answered by 25 Bxc6! Qxc6 26 d5! exd5 27 Qf4 △ Qb8† or Rxa5!) 24 Qf3 Nd8 25 d5! exd5 26 Bxd5 Qf5 27 Qe3 Rd7 28 Rad1 Bxf6 (Black is completely tied up in any case) 29 exf6 Ne6 30 Be4! Rxd1 31 Bxf5 Rxe1† 32 Qxe1 gxf5 33 Qe5 Kg8 34 Qg3† 1 - 0.

As a whole, 11...Qd7 is not so bad as this example indicates, mainly because of the subvariation 12 Be2 Bd5, when we have a lack of examples, but the play looks very double-edged. On the other hand, White's attacking chances throughout this chapter indicate that he needn't be afraid to play the gambit on this account.

1 d4	d5
2 c4	dxc4
3 Nf3	Nf6
4 Nc3	c6
5 e4	b5
6 e5	Nd5
7 a4	e6
8 axb5	Nxc3
9 bxc3	cxb5
10 Ng5	Bb7
11 Qh5	g6

The most popular move. Black judges that tempi are more important to him than the creation of weaknesses, but now he will have difficulties on the kingside.

12 Qg4

Diagram 61

After 12 Qg4

Now Black chooses: A 12...h6; B 12...Be7

Otherwise:

(a) 12...Nd7?! 13 Be2 Be7 transposed to 12...Be7 in two games, but here White should try 13 Rb1!, threatening 14 Rxb5 and 14 Bxc4. Then 13...Bxc6? 14 Nxe6! and 13...Qa5? 14 Qf4! are no good, so Black must give back the pawn;

(b) 12...Na6? 13 Rxa6! Bxa6 14 Qf3;

(c) 12...Bd5!? is reasonable, but has only been seen in one game, to my knowledge: 13 h4!? h6 (13...h5 14 Qf4 Qd7 ∞) 14 Ne4 Be7 15 Be2 Nc6 16 Bf3 (16 0-0!? △ Ba3 is an option) 16...Qd7 17 0-0 a5 18 Ba3!? (18 Bf4(!) would intend Nd6†) 18...h5 19 Qf4 Bxe4 20 Qxe4 Ra6 21 Bc1 Bd8 22 Ba3 Be7 23 Bc1 Bd8 24 Ba3 ½ - ½ Kasparov - Kakageldijev, USSR 1981.

Kasparov continued to play this line, however. Aside from the ideas indicated in the notes, White has 13 Qf4(!), e.g. 13...Qd7 14 Qf6 Rg8 15 Nxh7 Be7 16 Qf4 and one likes White. In case that doesn't appeal, 13 Be2 Be7 transposes to the line 12...Be7 13 Be2 Bd5 below.

A

12	h6
13 Ne4	

13 Nxe6? Qd7!.

13 .....   Nd7

The reader should note that, in this and similar positions, 13...Bxe4 14 Qxe4 Qd5 simply sets up the annoying Be2-f3 after White's queen moves, in this case by 15 Qf4.

14 Be2!?

White generally played this, but 14 Ba3!? Qa5 15 Bb2 Qb6 16 Be2 is also interesting. And 14 Rb1(!) could be a useful interpolation, considering the maneuver ...Qb6-c6 which follows.

14 .....   Bd5

14...a5 15 Rb1 (Ermolinsky); then 15...Bc6 16 Bf3 Qc8 17 0-0 △ Re1 and e.g. d5 with Nd6† is awkward for Black. 14...a5 15 0-0 Bd5 transposes to the next note.

15 0-0

Diagram 62   After 15 0-0

15 .....   Qb6

15...a5!? 16 Bf3 Qb6 17 Re1!? (17 Nd6†! Bxd6 18 Bxd5 exd5 19 exd6 Qxd6 [what else?] 20 Ba3 Qc6 21 Rfe1† – Ermolinsky) 17...Qc6! (17...Be7? 18 Nd6† is winning) 18 Qf4 Be7 19 h4 b4 20 cxb4 axb4 21 Rxa8† Qxa8 22 Nf6† Bxf6 (On 22...Nxf6 23 exf6 Bd8, the idea was 24 Qd6 Bxf3 25 Rxe6† fxe6 26 Qxe6† Kf8 27 Bf4! etc.) 23 Bxd5? (23 exf6 Bxf3 24 Qd6 Qd8 25 gxf3 Qxf6 26 Qxb4 "unclear" – *Schacknytt*) 23...Qxd5 24 exf6 c3 25 Qc7 0-0! 26 Bxh0 Ra8 and White's attack had run out in Svenn - Setterqvist, Swedish Ch 1984.

16 Bf3   Qc6!

Preventing the combination of the last note, which would follow on 16... a5: 17 Nd6†! Bxd6 18 Bxd5 etc..

17 Ba3   a5(?)

Better seems 17...Bxa3 18 Rxa3 0-0, when Black's kingside is weak, but he still has a pawn.

18 Nd6†   Bxd6
19 Bxd5   Qxd5
20 Bxd6

We are following Ermolinsky - Podgaets, USSR 1982. The threat is 21 Qh4 g5 22 Qh5 followed by f4, or first 21 f4. Black therefore tries 20...Nf6 21 exf6 Qxd6 22 Rfb1 0-0! (22...Qc6 23 Qf4 g5 24 Qe5 ±±) 23 Rxb5 Rfd8 24 Re5 ±/±. Black has pawn weaknesses and his kingside is dangerously vulnerable.

B

12	Be7
13 Be2	

After 13 h4!? h5 14 Qg3, the correct move seems to be 14...Bd5! (14...Nd7? 15 Nxe6; 14...Qd5 15 f3! △ Ne4 and Bg5; 14...Na6!? 15 Rb1 Qd7 16 Be2 Bd5 17 Bd1 Nc7 18 Bc2 unclear).

Diagram 63   After 13 Be2

13	Nd7

By far the main move. Black tries to get ...Nb6-d5 in as quickly as possible. But also very interesting is 13...Bd5!?. Then Saposhnikov - Sadomsky, correspondence 1958 went 14 Bf3 Nc6 15 Ne4!? (15 Bxd5!? Qxd5 16 Ne4 0-0-0! 17 Bh6 b4! unclear) 15...h5 (or perhaps just 15...b4, e.g. 16 Bh6 bxc3 17 Bg7 Rg8 unclear) 16 Qg3 b4! 17 0-0 Rb8!? 18 Bg5 Bxe4 19 Bxe4 Nxd4! 20 cxd4 Bxg5 21 d5! with complications leading to a draw. On 15 0-0, 15...a5 16 Bxd5 Qxd5 17 Ne4 b4! (17...h5 18 Qf4) 18 Rd1!? (18 cxb4 Qxd4; 18 Bg5? Bxg5 19 Nd6† Kd7) 18...0-0-0! looks okay for Black.

Another approach might be (13...Bd5:) 14 Ne4(!), e.g. 14...Nc6 (14...h5 15 Qf4! is no improvement) 15 Bh6 b4 (15...Bxe4 16 Qxe4 Qd5 17 Qg4 b4 18 Bf3 Qd7 19 0-0 b3 20 Rfd1) 16 Bg7 Rg8 17 Bf6 Bxe4 18 Qxe4 Qd5 19 Qf4 Bxf6 20 Bf3 Qd7 21 exf6 △21...bxc3 22 0-0 Rc8 23 Bxc6! Rxc6 24 d5! and the attack crashes through (e.g. 24...Qxd5 25 Qb8† Qd8 26 Qb5).

Of course this is all very messy, with many options for both sides.

14 Rb1(!)

The author's move. Otherwise:

(a) 14 h4!? h5 15 Qg3 Nb6 16 0-0 a5 (16...Bd5!?) 17 d5!? Nxd5 (17...Bxd5 18 Rd1 Qc7 19 Bf3 ∞ -- ECO; White has the burden of proof, although it is true that ...0-0 is prevented by Bxd5 and Nxe6) 18 Rd1 Qc7 19 Ne4! 0-0-0 20 Bg5 =/∞ Petrosian - Smyslov, USSR Ch 1951;

(b) 14 Bf3 has been the move for many years, but it's not clear whether this brings enough pressure to bear.

(See diagram on the next page)

True, 14...Qc7!? 15 Ne4 Nb6 (15...h5!? -- various) 16 Bh6 Rg8 17 Bg5 Bxe4 18 Bxe4 (±) 18...Nd5 (18...0-0-0 19 Ra5 b4 20 0-0 ±; 18...Rc8 19 0-0 Na4 20 Bxe7 Qxe7 21 Qf3 ± -- Pachman) 19 Bxd5 exd5 20 Bxe7 Qxe7 21 0-0 ± Geller - Unzicker, Stockholm 1952, is illustrative of White's advantages. Also 14...Bxf3!? 15 Qxf3 Bxg5 16 Bxg5 Qc8 17 Ra6! h6 18 Rc6

58

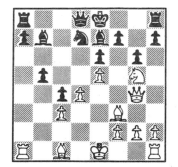

Diagram 64

After 14 Bf3

Qb8 19 Qh3 (△ Rxe6†) 19...Rh7 20 0-0 Nb6 21 Rxe6†! fxe6 22 Qxe6†
Kf8 23 Qxg6 Qb7 24 Bxh6† Rxh6 25 Qxh6† ± Povah - Hosking, Ramsgate
1981 was a fine exploitation of Black's weaknesses, and 25...Qg7 26 Qc6 Qd7
27 Qc5† Ke8 28 Re1! decided even *without* the advance of the 5(!) connect-
ed passed pawns.

But 14...Qc8! is hard to crack. For one thing, although 15 Ne4 has been
met by 15...0-0 (△ 16 Bh6? f5! ∓ -- various), even more convincing was the direct 15 Ne4 f5! 16 exf6 Nxf6 17 Nxf6† Bxf6 18 Bxb7 (18 Bh6! ∓) 18...
Qxb7 19 Qxe6† Qe7 ∓ Szabo - Petrosian, Moscow - Budapest 1955, e.g. 20
Ra6 Qxe6† 21 Rxe6† Kf7 22 Ra6 Rhe8† 23 Be3 Re6 etc.. Here better practical chances are offered by 15 h4! h5 16 Qg3 (16 Qf4!? Bxg5 17 hxg5 Bxf3
18 Qxf3 Nb6 19 Rh4 [△g4] 19...Rg8 20 d5!? Nxd5 21 Ba3 Qa6 22 Rf4
Rg7 Rogers - Kostic, Kraljevo 1984 is given as "unclear" by *Informant*, but
Black's material seems the most important factor), with the idea 16...Nb6 17
Ba3! (17 Ne4?! Bxe4 18 Bxe4 Nd5; 17 0-0 Bxf3 18 Qxf3 Bxg5) 17...Bxa3
18 Rxa3, as I gave in my original article. Black has many defensive tries, however, e.g. 16...a5 (to cut off the White bishop by ...b4).

14 Rb1 wins a tempo for the attack which comes in very useful later.

14 .....   Bc6

Versus Rxb5 and Bxc4. The other idea is 14...Bxg5!? 15 Bxg5 Qa5, but
16 0-0 Bd5 17 Bf3! Nb6!? 18 Qf4 (±/±) 18...f5 (only move) 19 exf6 0-0
20 Bg4! was great for White in Watson - Orton, San Jose 1984: 20...Na4!?
21 Rae1 Rae8 22 Qd6 Qb6 23 Qd7 Qb7 24 f7† and White won in a few
moves.

15 Bf3   Qc8

Certainly not 15...Bxf3? 16 Qxf3 ± or 15...Qc7 16 Rxb5!. Better 15...
Qb6!? 16 0-0 Qb7 (16...Bd5 17 Bxd5 exd5 18 e6), but then 17 Ne4! △ Bg5
(or Re1 and Bg5 or Nd6†) is quite promising.

16 0-0

(See diagram on the next page)

This position is critical for an assessment of 11...g6. Let's look at some
ideas:

(a) 16...Nb6?! 17 Ne4, and the desirable 17...Bxe4 18 Bxe4 merely loses the
b-pawn;

(b) 16...h5?! 17 Qh3 Nb6 18 Ne4 Nd5 19 Bg5!;

Diagram 65   After 16 0-0

(c) **16...0-0!?** was played in Watson - Bohn, Rohnert Park 1985: 17 Re1 a5 (compare 16...a5 below) 18 d5! exd5 (18...Bxd5? 19 Bxd5 exd5 20 e6 Nf6 21 exf7† [21 Qh3] 21...Rxf7 22 Qxc8† Rxc8 23 Nxf7 Kxf7 24 Rxb5) 19 e6!? (If 19 Qd4!? △ 19...Qd8 20 Nxf7, 19...Nc5! 20 Bxd5 Ne6! is equal. Correct is 19 Nxf7!, with advantage -- compare 16...a6 below: '(e2)') 19...Nf6 20 exf7† (20 Qd4!?) 20...Rxf7 21 Qd4 Ne4! (Otherwise e.g. 21...Qd7 22 Nxf7 Kxf7 23 Bg5 △23...b4 24 Rxe7†! Qxe7 25 Bxf6 Qxf6 26 Bxd5† etc.; or 21...Rg7 22 Bf4! and now 22...Ne4 23 Nxe4 dxe4 24 Bxe4 or 22...Qd7 23 Re5! △ Rbe1) 22 Nxf7 Kxf7 23 Bxe4 dxe4, and at this point White didn't get anywhere with 24 Rxb5!?, but slower moves such as 24 Bh6 Bf6 25 Qe3 a4 are dangerous only for him. Thus 19 Nxf7! should have been tried.

(d) **16...a5** 17 Re1 is a similar idea, but if Black wants to avoid transposition by 17...0-0, 17...Nb6? 18 Ne4! is not the way to do it, and in general he must be careful about d5.

(e) **16...a6(!)** is probably the most logical move, but also illustrates White's attacking ideas after 17 Re1:

Diagram 66   After 17 Re1

(e1) **17...Nb6!?** 18 Bxc6(!) Qxc6 19 Ne4 Nd5 (19...0-0-0 20 Qf3!, hitting f7) 20 Bg5 Bf8!? (20...0-0-0 21 Bxe7 Nxe7 22 Nd6† Rxd6 23 exd6 Nd5 [22...Qxd6 23 Qf3! ±] 24 Qf3 and Black is tied up due to 24...Rf8 25 Rxe6! or e.g. 24...Qd7 25 Ra1 Kb7 26 Re5 etc.) 21 Nf6†! Nxf6 22 Bxf6 Rg8

(See diagram on the next page)

23 d5!! exd5!? (23...Qxd5 24 Rbd1 Qc6 [24...Qb7 25 Qh4! △25...h5 26 Rd4!] 25 Qd4 Qc7 26 Re2 △ Red2 etc.) 24 e6 Bg7 (what else?) 25 Bxg7!

Diagram 67

After 22...Rg8

Rxg7 26 Qd4! Kf8 (26...Rg8 27 Qf6 ±±) 27 e7† Kg8 28 Qxd5! ±±.

(e2) (from Diagram 66:) 17...0-0 18 d5! (18 Qh3!? is also very interesting: 18...Bxg5 19 Bxg5 Bxf3 20 Qxf3 Rb8? 21 Re3! △ Qf4 and Bf6, but here 20...Nb6 may hold. 20 Ne4!?) 18...exd5 (18...Bxd5!? 19 Bxd5 exd5 20 Nxf7!? Nc5! 21 e6 Ne4 22 Bh6 with attack, e.g. 22...Rxf7 23 exf7† Kxf7 24 Rxe4! dxe4 25 Qxe4 and 26 Re1, or 22...Bc5 23 Rxe4! dxe4 24 Qxe4 etc.) 19 Nxf7! Rxf7 (19...Nc5 20 e6 △20...Nd3? 21 Qd4!, and otherwise 21 Bh6) 20 e6 ±, e.g. 20...Rg7 21 exd7 Bxd7 22 Bxd5† Kh8 23 Qd4 Bc5 24 Qh4 Ra7 25 Bh6 etc..

Note that the bulk of '(a)' through '(e)' above is purely analysis, and quite possibly not "the whole truth" about this line with 11...g6 and 12...Be7. I have included it in lieu of over-the-board examples to illustrate what I believe to be the key tactical ideas.

In general, this main-line attack for White has been seriously underestimated by the theoreticians, and Kasparov's use of the e4 gambit will certainly attract attention. At the risk of boring the reader, I should repeat that White's attack versus 4...c6 is by no means so well worked out as that versus 4...a6, and many questions remain. But it certainly seems an exciting and positive way of confronting this traditionally stolid defense.

Index of Variations

I. 1 d4 d5 2 c4 dxc4 3 Nf3   6
    3...Nd7   6
    3...c6   6
    3...e6   6
  3...Bg4   6
  3...c5   8
  3...b5   9
  3...a6   10
    4 e4 b5 5 a4 Bb7 6 axb5 axb5 7 Rxa8 Bxa8 8 Nc3
    8...e6   12
    8...c6   13

II. 1 d4 d5 2 c4 dxc4 3 Nf3 Nf6 4 Nc3   15
    4...Nbd7   15
    4...Nc6   15
  4...Bf5   16
  4...e6   16
    5 e4 Bb4 6 Bg5
    6...h6   17
    6...b5   18
    6...c5   19
  4...c5   21

III. 1 d4 d5 2 c4 dxc4 3 Nf3 Nf6 4 Nc3 a6 5 e4 b5 6 e5 Nd5 7 a4 26
    7...Bf5   26
    7...b4   26
  7...Bb7   26
  7...Nb4   28

IV. 1 d4 d5 2 c4 dxc4 3 Nf3 Nf6 4 Nc3 a6 5 e4 b5 6 e5 Nd5
  7 a4 c6   32
  8 axb5 Nxc3 9 bxc3 cxb5 10 Ng5 f6 11 Qf3 Ra7 12 e6
  12...Qb6   33
    13 d5 fxg5
    14 Qf7†   33
    14 Be3   34
  12...Bb7   35

V. 1 d4 d5 2 c4 dxc4 3 Nf3 Nf6 4 Nc3 a6 5 e4 b5 6 e5 Nb5

    7 a4 Nxc3 8 bxc3   38

    8...Qd5 9 g3   38

      9...Be6   38

      9...Bb7 10 Bg2 Qd7   40

        11 Ba3   40

        11 Nh4   44

    8...Bb7 9 e6   45

      9...fxe6   45

      9...f6   46

VI. 1 d4 d5 2 c4 dxc4 3 Nf3 Nf6 4 Nc3 c6   49

    5 e4 b5 6 e5 Nd5 7 a4 Bf5   49

VII. 1 d4 d5 2 c4 dxc4 3 Nf3 Nf6 4 Nc3 c6 5 e4 b5 6 e5 Nd5

    7 a4 e6   52

VIII. 1 d4 d5 2 c4 dxc4 3 Nf3 Nf6 4 Nc3 c6 5 e4 b5 6 e5 Nd5

    7 a4 e6 8 axb5 Nxc3 9 bxc3 cxb5 10 Ng5 Bb7 11 Qh5 g6

    12 Qg4   56

    12...h6   56

    12...Be7   58

Fine Books From Chess Enterprises

Openings:

Druash: Alapin's Opening	$3.50
Eckert: Sicilian Scheveningen: Keres' Attack	$5.50
Estrin: Gambits	$5.00
Estrin: Three Double King Pawn Openings	$5.00
Estrin: Wilkes-Barre Variation, Two Knights Defense	$4.00
Grefe & Silman: Center Counter	$5.50
Filipowicz & Konikowski: 4...d5 in the Cordel Defense	$3.25
Kapitaniak: Sicilian Defense, Wing Gambits	$5.00
Koltanowski: Colle System, 11th Edition	$5.50
Konikowski: Tartakower System, Queen's Gambit	$5.00
Konikowski: Petrosian System, Queen's Indian Defense	$6.50
Leverett: Sicilian Defense, Velimirovic Attack	$5.00
Marfia: Queen's Gambit With Bf4	$2.50
Marfia: Queen's Indian With 4 g3	$3.50
Marfia & Dudley: Double Fianchetto Opening System	$2.00
Schiller: Cambridge Springs Defense, Queen's Gambit	$6.00
Schiller: Catalan	$5.50
Schiller: Gruenfeld Defense, Russian Variations	$5.50
Schiller: Sicilian: Modern Richter Rauzer	$5.50
Schiller: Orthodox Variation, Qu een's Gambit	$6.50
Taylor: Rubinstein Variation, Nimzo-Indian Defense	$5.00
Tejler & Marfia: Euwe Defense, Blackmar-Diemer Gambit	$2.50
Wall: 300 King's Gambit Miniatures	$2.95
Wall: 500 French Miniatures	$5.00
Wall: 500 Queen's Gambit Miniatures	$5.00
Wall: 500 Sicilian Miniatures	$5.00
Watson: 4 Nc3 Gambit in the Queen's Gambit Accepted & Slav	$5.00
Watson: Taimanov & Knight's Tour Benoni	$5.00
Watson: 6...Nc6 in the Saemisch Variation, King's Indian	$5.00
Williams: The Real American Wilkes-Barre	$3.25

Middle Game:

Nimzowitsch: Blockade	$4.50
Sheffield: Tension in the Chess Position	$4.00

Endgame:

Botvinnik: Botvinnik on the Endgame	$5.50
Brieger: The Joy of Mate	$2.00
Cvetkov: Pawn Endings	$5.00
Mednis: Practical Rook Endings	$4.50

Games, Bibliography:

Botvinnik: Fifteen Games and Their Stories	$4.95
Koltanowski: Chessnicdotes I	$5.00
Koltanowski: Chessnicdotes II	$5.00
Platz: Chess Memoirs	$10.00

Tournaments:

Christiansen: 1980 U. S. Championship	$5.00
Christiansen: 1981 U. S. Championship	O/P
Christiansen: 1983 U. S. Championship	$6.50
Fine: Amsterdam 1936	$3.50
Marfia: 1981 U. S. Open Palo Alto	$5.00
Marfia & Watson: 1982 U. S. Open St Paul	$5.00
Marfia & Watson: 1983 U. S. Open Pasadena	$6.00
Marfia: 1984 U. S. Open Ft Worth	$5.50
Marfia: 1985 U. S. Open Hollywood, Florida	$5.50
Hebert: Border Wars III, North American Correspondence Championship	$5.00

Chess Problems:

Barclay: America Salutes Comins Mansfield	$5.00

Comics:

Watson: Chessman Comics 2, Treachery in Transylvania	$2.50

Chess Enterprises, Inc.
107 Crosstree
Coraopolis, PA 15108